PRAISE FOR

THE SOCIAL MEDIA SIDE DOOR

"Any reader can take this book, apply Ian's suggestions, and immediately start getting results from their social media marketing efforts, either for themselves or their employers. In fact, their Klout score will go up, too. It's one of the most informative and effective social media books I've ever read."

—JOE FERNANDEZ, CEO and cofounder of Klout

"Social media is about connections. Real, personal connections that open doors, change your career, and help you win. Ian Greenleigh will teach you exactly how to take it from theory to reality."

—ANDY SERNOVITZ, author of *Word of Mouth Marketing*

"This is the stuff you wish you had known all along about social media. Greenleigh's mix of personal experience and proven strategy make this a compelling—and remarkably useful—read."

—MACK COLLIER, author of *Think Like a Rock Star*
and founder of #blogchat

"There's a whole other mode of using social media in marketing—particularly in business-to-business, professional services, and in any business where thought leadership is effective: influencer marketing. In *The Social Media Side Door*, Ian Greenleigh has provided a thorough and valuable guide to overcome obstacles and be more effective. The timing couldn't be better."

—RIC DRAGON, author of *Social Marketology*
and cofounder and CEO of DragonSearch

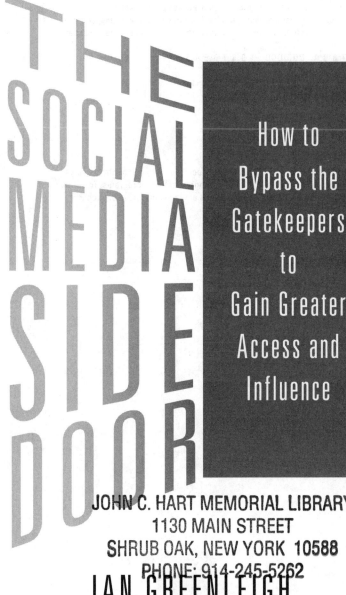

THE SOCIAL MEDIA SIDE DOOR

How to Bypass the Gatekeepers to Gain Greater Access and Influence

IAN GREENLEIGH

Mc Graw Hill Education

New York   Chicago   San Francisco   Athens   London   Madrid
Mexico City   Milan   New Delhi   Singapore   Sydney   Toronto

1 2 3 4 5 6 7 8 9 0   DOC/DOC   1 9 8 7 6 5 4 3

ISBN   978-0-07-181673-1
MHID   0-07-181673-9

e-ISBN   978-0-07-181674-8
e-MHID   0-07-181674-7

McGraw-Hill Education books are available at special quantity discounts to use as premiums and sales promotions or for use in corporate training programs. To contact a representative, please visit the Contact Us pages at www.mhprofessional.com.

To Merideth, with whom I share
the tiny moments

CONTENTS

ACKNOWLEDGMENTS

When someone takes a chance on you, you don't hesitate. That's the story of this book, essentially: a series of remarkable people ignoring conventions, and, probably, their better judgment, to give me a chance.

The team at Bazaarvoice did just that when they hired me, and never once in more than three years did they pull me back to earth or tell me to quit dreaming. Deb de Freitas, Amber Quist, Sam Decker, Lisa Pearson, Erin Nelson, Amy Hayes, Brett Hurt, and Brant Barton—thank you.

I'm enormously grateful to those who provided early feedback, essential introductions, advance praise, guidance, and other generous acts, especially Mack Collier, Brian Solis, Ann Handley, Simon Salt, Andy Sernovitz, Jay Baer, Seth Godin, Joe Fernandez, Chris Heuer, Ekaterina Walter, Ric Dragon, and Rohit Bhargava.

The people I interviewed helped make this book infinitely more interesting. They include Clay Shirky, Brian Stelter, Marcy Massura, Teddy Goff, Greg Galant, Ryan Holiday, Jane Levy, and Alex Howard.

My agent, Linda Langton, immediately saw this book's potential, as did Casey Ebro at McGraw-Hill. Thanks for seeing something in a first-time author.

This would still be an unfulfilled dream were it not for the family and friends in Texas and California who supported me all the way. My wife, Merideth, never doubted this day would come. Neither did my parents, who quite literally decided while I was in the womb that I would one day be an author. And lastly, my sister Elise, who has followed her passion and filled me with pride.

Thank you all for taking a chance on me.

My Story

'll never forget walking out of that mall, proud of myself for nailing the job interview at a cell phone kiosk. What's more embarrassing than not getting that job—I didn't even get a callback, and it stung— is the fact that I was so close to settling for it.

It was early 2010, and I wanted to make the jump from salesperson to marketer. I had almost no on-paper experience in marketing, and my résumé was far from impressive. That cell phone kiosk job was the first interview I had, and I went to it because I had begun to doubt whether anyone would give me a chance in marketing. I was running out of money and confidence.

A few days later, still feeling pretty hopeless about my situation— why, I again wondered, did I major in political science?—I found a blog post about a young PR job seeker named Grant Turck. He had targeted the agencies he wanted to work for with Facebook ads, and he was getting some interest from them, as well as publicity from well-known bloggers. I decided to give Grant a call, and he was happy to walk me through his strategy.

Even before the first click, I felt a renewed optimism. I was doing something different, something only a handful of people had tried—ever. My Facebook ad targeted marketing managers and C-level executives in Austin, mentioned the fact that I was "looking for a job in new media," and finished with, "Can you help? Click here."

I put together a special Hire Me page on my blog, linked to it from my ad, and waited.

It started with a few blog comments from well-wishers like this one:

I want to work for you.

I'm Ian. I'm a nominee for the 2010 TX Social Media Award and I'm looking for a job in new media. Can you help? Click here.

👍 Like

I was totally impressed with your Facebook ad and I had to let you know. You have my respect and gung-ho wishes for great success with it.

Next I received four separate comments offering me freelance work, and I got a handful of e-mails promising to connect me to companies that were looking for talent. Within a week, I was talking to hiring managers, setting up interviews, and getting consulting inquiries. It was working. I promised myself I wouldn't settle for the first offer on the table.

Three weeks and less than $200 in ad fees later, I had multiple offers to choose from, all of which were infinitely better than that damned cell phone kiosk job. Thanks to those unexpected freelance inquiries, I had options—the most important of which was the option to hold out on accepting any offer short of *exactly* what I was looking for. While weighing which offer to accept, I got a call about a job I had previously applied for but for which I had been quickly screened out.

It was perfect for me: a social media manager position at Bazaarvoice, my top pick of employers. The company has always had a reputation both for being extremely picky about whom it interviews and for being rigorous in its selection process—exactly the kind of earned exclusivity that attracts competitive top performers in the first place. In fact, when career site Glassdoor ranked the top 25 most difficult companies to interview, based on data from "80,000 interview reviews," Bazaarvoice came in at #14, beating out *legendarily* tough gigs like Facebook (#24), Teach for America (#16), and Amazon (#25). Needless to say, I wasn't surprised when I initially heard no from the company. But I *was* surprised—and thrilled—to get called back in.

I had written about wanting to work for Bazaarvoice in a blog post about using social ads in my job hunt, and the CMO had seen it after my post had triggered a Google Alert for the company name and sent him an automated e-mail. Several interviews and a test presentation later, I had my dream job.

Writing about the experience brought me some attention and has also helped a lot of other dispirited job seekers. But I had stumbled onto something much bigger than a new job-hunting technique. I had found an entirely different way of doing things, an alternative path to achievement in almost any realm. Why stop there?

What I found was a social media side door, a way around the barriers that pose constant threats to our forward progress. I later realized that I had found these side doors before but hadn't recognized them as such. In my previous sales work, I had been using my active social media presence to reach prospects that were otherwise unreachable. Before that, working in the soul-crushing field of collections, I had honed a detectivelike knack for tracking down and reaching out to people who knew better than to pick up the phone or return my e-mails. And now, working in marketing, I've used these same principles to engage with C-level business decision makers who control billion-dollar marketing and advertising budgets. I've been able to interview some of the most sought-after business thinkers of our time. My ideas have been featured in *Harvard Business Review, Ad Age,* and many other gold-list outlets, and I've written for many of the top blogs in the world. It wasn't *supposed* to happen like this, but it continues to happen because I keep discovering new social media side doors to explore.

Social media side doors have opened everywhere. Through them, we have the unique ability to earn the attention of people and organizations that are bombarded every day by countless requests for attention and consideration—résumés, e-mails, phone calls, invitations, meetings, and more. These messages fight it out just to fly coach on standby, and they rarely make it past security. Our messages board private jets and fly direct to their destinations, where they are escorted past customs and placed immediately into the hands of their intended recipients. Or something like that.

Through these side doors, a universe of opportunity exists that few people are even aware of. You don't learn this stuff in business school or from career counselors. Spotting these doors has nothing to do with the skills you've inherited, your station in life, or the balance in your bank account.

The delta between our aspirations and reality might be wide, but social media offers us more ways than ever to navigate it—if we can find the side doors. It sure beats the hell out of pushing cell phones at the mall.

My job is to explain how these side doors are changing our world and to show you how to discover them for yourself.

Your job is to walk through them before they are overrun and boarded up and to use the skills you learn in this book to locate and build new side doors.

We'll talk to some truly fascinating individuals on both sides of the door and learn how access and influence have changed forever.

This book will leave you with a deeper understanding of three things:

1. The ways in which social media has rewritten the rules of access and influence (and what's next)
2. The larger significance of these fundamental shifts

3. The things you must do to identify and open social media side doors

While certain sections of this book will apply most intuitively to one audience or another, every chapter contains knowledge that is broadly applicable. Although I frequently draw on examples from my own experience, and I use specific contexts like job seeking and earning media coverage to illustrate key points, the majority of the techniques and strategies in *The Social Media Side Door* can be useful within many different contexts and in pursuit of a wide range of goals.

This book should spark discussions, questions, stories, and ideas. As you read it, please share your thoughts with other readers and me (@be3d) by using the hashtag #tsmsd on Twitter and Facebook (make sure the post is public). Think of it as a real-time book club. Let's connect.

CHAPTER 1

Gatekeeping and Access

The First 3,000 Telephones

Mr. Watson, come here! I want to see you!
  —ALEXANDER GRAHAM BELL,
    March 10, 1876 (the world's first phone call)

inviting coworkers
  —JACK DORSEY,
    March 21, 2006 (the world's first tweet)[1]

Shortly after a new communications medium arrives, side doors of access are created by the confluence of low adoption and technological immaturity. These side doors do not last forever. The excitement and the mutual opportunity that initially pass through them eventually become costly—and sometimes a liability. The fortunate few who discover these doors get in early and make out like bandits before the rest of the world finds out. Side doors soon become crowded and unreliable, while the people who originally left them open see no choice but to seal them against the oncoming crowds.

Social media has created an incredible array of side doors, and all of them remain open—if you know where to look. Right now, social media is the telephone before there were secretaries and voice mail. It's e-mail before spam and autoreplies. History tells us that this degree of access is not sustainable, and side doors don't stay open. Sometime soon, we'll be telling "remember-when" stories. It's up to you: do you want to be the storyteller, recalling how good the social media side doors were for you, or do you want to be the audience, wishing you had known—and acted?

One year after Bell invented the telephone, the world had 3,000 working telephones.[2] Think about the calls placed to and from those first 3,000 telephones, the excitement with which they were placed and received, and the elite circle that one instantly entered just by placing one of them. A person could connect with those who were all but unreachable by other means, an exclusive channel of access that opened up for these early adopters alone—a technological side door.

The normal rules of polite society would, of course, apply to early telephone communication—no foul language, no harassment or violations of privacy. But outside these limitations, one would have free rein to explore a brand-new communications channel. The voices on the other end were no doubt tinged with the excitement of early adoption. Most calls were between familiar parties, and the telephone was a new way for existing contacts to connect. For the most part, it helped maintain and build relationships, not start them.

Doubters, Evangelists, and Opportunists

There were certainly a lot of doubters of the telephone's potential. Among them was Western Union, which dismissed the technology in an 1876 internal memo: "The telephone has too many shortcomings to be seriously considered as a means of communication. The device is inherently of no value to us."[3] On the other end of the spectrum, there were early evangelists, who trumpeted the telephone's invention without much evidence of its eventual success—some of history's lucky guessers. In between the two extremes were the early adopters, who focused on the telephone's utility at the time and stayed out of the predictions business.

This is where we find the opportunists throughout history. They're busy putting the technology of the day to work for them. Whoever made the world's first sales call was among this group. I imagine this person taking a deep breath as the operator connected him to his intended prospect. The recipient answers, expecting a familiar voice, only to find a stranger on the other end. An exchange of greetings and then the moment of truth. Does the prospect hang up or cut the conversation short? Or does the prospect sit and listen to what the stranger has to say? I suspect it's the latter. The recipient has no concept of phone solicitation. It probably hasn't yet dawned on the listener that this new network could even be used to conduct business between people or firms. To the prospect, the person on the other end of the call is not a nuisance but a member of a limited circle in which having access to a connected telephone is the sole qualification. And people do business with those in their circle, even if the circle was entered through a side door.

When the telephone enters mass production and prices drop, and as a national telephone network is built, the circle widens. The exclusive privileges of circle membership wither away, and the cost of being accessed shifts in a way that repeats itself each time a successful new communications technology climbs the adoption curve. The party seeking access is able to find it more cheaply and easily than ever before. The party being accessed begins to find this access problematic, and the side door starts to swing shut.

Exclusive No More

It isn't the work of an elite cabal with grand designs on limiting access; instead it's a gradual, decentralized process that begins whenever this access becomes problematic in the eyes of those granting it. Consider what happens next. New Haven, Connecticut, receives the first phone book in 1878, which contains fewer than 50 listings.[4] In 1894, Bell's patents expire, allowing new companies to enter the telephone production business.[5] Six years later, in 1900, 1.35 million telephone lines can be found in the United States, and Americans are making nearly 8 million calls per day.[6] Before sales calls were established, marketers were using phone books to locate the most qualified prospects for mailers. JNP Cramer, president of Multi-Mailing Co., tells *Printer's Ink* in 1903, "The rural telephone sorts out the influential classes in every community, and lists of names made up from telephones are excellent for high-class propositions."[7] In 1935, Willy Müller invents the first automatic answering machine.[8] At some point along the way, secretaries begin to screen calls. Unlisted numbers are offered to those who cannot be bothered. The circle of access expands rapidly with the rise of telephone use, and what was once a proud, exclusive club becomes a free-for-all.

Understanding the Gatekeepers

Trailing not far behind the introduction of a successful new communications technology are the human and technological gatekeepers. Human gatekeepers include receptionists, executive assistants, recruiters, bureaucrats, budget managers, script readers—anyone who has the power to slow, stop, or accelerate access to someone or something. These gatekeepers are used to taking messages that they'll never actually relay, used to deciding whether inquiries are worth the attention of the people they work for, and, above all else, used to saying "no" and "not interested." Their ultimate charter as gatekeepers is to keep the people who are paid to focus on important things from having to make hundreds of tiny decisions every day that threaten to derail productivity. It's easy to see this work from a cynic's perspective. After all, these are people who are paid to stop others from getting through. But the reality is more nuanced. Great work requires sustained concentration and the ability to devote high-level resources to the projects and tasks that merit this attention. Everything else can be more efficiently dealt with by subordinates or no one at all. Making those calls is a necessary role, and probably thankless.

While it still plays a big part in society and business, human gatekeeping needs to be supplemented or replaced by technological gatekeeping in order for organizations to scale. Some technological gatekeeping is put in place to hide or remove public information. The CEO's direct line can't be listed on the company website, and his or her e-mail address shouldn't be something easily guessed, like firstname.lastname@companyname.com. The Radicati Group finds that while the average number of business e-mails received per day is tracking upward, the average number of spam e-mails received is plateauing, thanks in part to automated filtering.[9] This gatekeeping comes at a significant cost, however, as the same report found that medium-size to large companies are each spending millions fighting spam.

Social media is giving a voice to some of the smallest populations on the planet, most of which have few dedicated media providers printing or broadcasting in their native languages or covering topics of direct interest to them. IndigenousTweets.com indexes data about tweets and Twitter users in nearly 150 "indigenous and minority languages" from around the world. The site's profile for the Asturian language, a native language for some in the Asturias region of Spain, lists 738 users and 191,539 individual tweets.[10] These Twitter users hail from some of the most marginalized and disenfranchised groups in the world, and yet they have found a way to connect and engage in the new media landscape, the most remarkable feature of which is the *absence* of barriers. In the words of Kevin Scannel, the professor who leads the effort:

[Social media have] allowed sometimes-scattered communities to connect and use their languages online in a natural way. Social media have also been important in engaging young people, who are the most important demographic in language revitalization efforts. Together we're breaking down the idea that only global languages like English and French have a place online!

Early Adoption and Social Adstock

The technology adoption life cycle has been studied exhaustively ever since Everett Rogers developed his famous Rogers bell curve in 1962.[11] As more of a population adopts a technology, adoption becomes less expensive. However, as a communications technology edges closer to saturation, other costs emerge for its early users. Increased activity volume requires more attention and follow-up. The exclusivity that once appealed to early users—and the related benefits of being in an elite circle—all but disappears. As more people start using the innovation, access is given to anyone and everyone. This is when gatekeeping kicks in as a set of tools and practices that preserve the value of the innovation while reducing the costs associated with being accessed more easily.

Most decision makers aren't actually early adopters, and they're usually not even in the early majority of users when looking at total adoption. But they can be considered early users within their peer group. Executives, for instance, actually tend to lag behind the general population in personal social media use. Of the Fortune 500 CEOs, only about 19 are active on Twitter—less than 4 percent, compared with 34 percent of the U.S. population.[12,13]

Let's consider one Fortune 500 CEO's use of social media. Jack Salzwedel of American Family Mutual Insurance Group has tweeted thousands of times; he has over 2,000 followers, and he is mentioned seven times per day, on average. He's extremely engaged with AmFam-proud employees on Twitter, and not only does he respond to their tweets, but he chimes in about everything from the weather to books to sports.

But what happens when 7 mentions per day shoot up to 20? Or 78 (the average number of e-mails received by corporate users daily)?[14] Being accessed becomes burdensome when the number is big enough.

Adstock is a way of talking about advertising's influence on what we buy.[15] At its most basic level, repeated exposure to advertising rapidly increases awareness, until the rate of awareness building first slows due to saturation and then plateaus. A similar effect can be found in social media, but the effect permeates more than just influence. Let's call it social media decay. Social media decay occurs on both the individual and systemic levels. When a user first ventures into social media, every event seems significant. Friend requests, Twitter mentions, LinkedIn messages, blog comments—these are all events that excite for hours due to their relative infrequency at the early stages of social media use. There is also the payoff aspect; the effort we've been putting into building a blog readership or into growing our Twitter networks is starting to yield a return. My first few blog posts received almost zero interactions. Then, on my fourth or fifth, out of the ether, a blog comment appeared. I remember how it felt—like it was all up from there. This one positive interaction resonated throughout my entire day, and I could barely wait to write another post and see what would happen next. You'll see this degree of excitement lead to a lot of sad exchanges with spammers on early-stage blogs. An automated spambot will leave a generic, barely intelligible comment like this one from "Dentist Barry," pulled from the spam filter on my blog:

> *Hello your website is great .I am with your side that you are making your horizontical knowledge.I would love to know more of your site.Will come back!*

And the new bloggers, bless their souls, will approve the comment and leave enthusiastic replies:

So glad you liked it, Barry! Thanks for your kind words, and
I hope you like my next post, too!

But the real comments and social interactions keep you going, making you hungry for more. The follower and friend counts climb alongside the number of retweets.

Shutting Off the Fire Hose

At a certain point—different for everyone—you become saturated with activity. Influence over your actions and thinking, ease of access, and level of engagement begin to taper off.

Influence starts to diminish in that each piece of content, interaction, or social contact holds less power to influence your behavior; it's competing with more and more demands for your attention, and it's less likely to be the basis for any action on your part. For example, say we're looking for a new vendor. We ask our Facebook friends (or Twitter followers or LinkedIn connections) for recommendations. The power of each recommendation to ultimately influence our selection is greater when we're relatively new to social media, and that power gets weaker over time due to volume. Two recommendations are easy to research. Twenty recommendations are not.

We also put less stock in social signals as time goes on. It's not necessarily cynicism—rather it's more of a realism that takes hold with regard to our perception of the motivations of others across the social web. When we're new to the world of social media, we're amazed at how friendly everyone is, even if we find the prevalence of hyperbole and multiple exclamation points a bit odd. Hang around long enough, and we will have been on the other end of a few bad sales pitches that start as social interactions. Maybe we meet someone offline, at a conference, and we're surprised at the incongruity between the person's social media and offline personalities. These things happen more frequently the longer we spend in social media, and they eventually dispel some of the naiveté we had toward the intentions of others, including the extent to which we should trust what they say, what they recommend—and even who they say they are. It's a process that leads us to a healthy, mature understanding: people are still people on the social web.

Recalibrating Access

A reduction of access is another natural consequence of social media maturity. Part of this is due simply to information overload. Too many inputs, not enough processing power, not enough time. Keeping up with what our social contacts are doing and saying is not without costs, and when those costs become too much, it's time to regulate the flow of information. We can do this by trimming our connections, defriending, unfollowing. We can also adjust the settings of our social networks by telling Facebook, for instance, that we don't want updates from our crazy cat-lady cousin appearing in our feed. The other reasons we typically limit access to ourselves concern privacy and abuse. After a few phone calls or e-mails from people we don't care to interact with through those channels, we'll hide our contact information. More nefarious—but all too common—are phishing scams that use social media to propagate and exploit access.

The flow of inputs is tapered off, and our use of social media starts to look more like our use of e-mail. We don't read everything aimed at us. We respond to things selectively. The name in the "from" field helps us judge how much attention to devote to the message. Senders we recognize and value will get our attention. Those we don't, won't, unless they catch us in the rare moment where curiosity and free time intersect. This is social media decay, and it's a part of the journey for people who spend enough of their time online. It's also something that anyone trying to access them will need to learn how to deal with.

Media Gatekeepers: Not Dead Yet

Some gatekeeping occurs without the people behind the gate ever knowing it. Controlling the flow of information is one of the oldest forms of gatekeeping. Media outlets choose which programs and content to air, newspapers choose what to print, and the audience traditionally has no say in these decisions. Information that is of high value may never reach us, and in the old media environment, the best we could hope for was that at least *some of it does*. Social media has radically changed both distribution and consumption. It amplifies our ability to reach and influence people with information, and it is not constrained by the same level of media gatekeeping.

Information gatekeepers are losing the war to control the stream. But they're still powerful; they still have their jobs. Let me be clear here that I'm not alleging any conspiracies (at least in the free world); I'm not going to tell you that a powerful elite holds an iron grip on information to willfully disadvantage the masses or to shape our reality. Certainly, our reality is shaped by what we see and hear, but this is a consequence of nature and not an elaborate scheme for our minds and obedience. Even in the historically oppressed corners of the world, in which information *is* subject to control by an "elaborate scheme" of censors and other apparatchiks, people are finding ways to connect. To them, social media is more escape hatch than side door.

Interestingly, the fact that you and I can access a vast, digital universe of conspiracy theories (and the fact that the loony-bin conspiracy website *Infowars* ranks among the top 500 websites in the United States) is a testament to how wide the cracks in the information barriers are getting.

But why did barriers exist in the first place? The gatekeepers have a few goals that are worth considering.

First, gatekeepers can serve as filters for truth and accuracy. By stanching the flow of bad information and only releasing information after careful and thorough vetting, gatekeepers ostensibly make sure the inputs to our worldview, beliefs, and resulting decisions are based on their controlled information output of "better" information. This might be called "paternalism by filtering."

Second, gatekeepers aim to steer the public's collective focus toward what matters rather than toward things that are trivial, irrelevant, or inconsequential. A classic example of this role is the media's handling of John F. Kennedy's sex life. As Alicia C. Shepard wrote in *American Journalism Review*:

> It used to be so simple back in the days when John F. Kennedy was president. What reporters covering the White House knew about his promiscuity never saw its way into print. It just wasn't considered relevant.[16]

Third, gatekeepers may control the flow of information in an attempt to shape outcomes. In other words, traditional media might *actively* try to push content that supports a particular agenda—a step beyond bias by omission to bias by inclusion.

You're likely familiar with the case of Trayvon Martin, the unarmed, black teenager who was shot and killed by a neighborhood watch captain in an Orlando suburb on February 26, 2012.[17] Subsequent evidence, including tragic 911 recordings, suggests that the shooting was, in fact, a coldblooded murder. It seems that Martin was buying Skittles and threatening nobody. The jury disagreed and acquitted the shooter, George Zimmerman. That's the sad story you know. But there's another story here about media gatekeeping.

Black media was quick to pick up this story of alleged racial violence, as were local news outlets.[18] But it wasn't until the story was cascading through the social web, the subject of hundreds of thousands of Facebook posts and tweets for weeks, that it garnered the attention of the national, mainstream media. The discrepancy between social and mainstream pickup is a telling one. Decision makers at mainstream outlets seem to have originally decided that the story didn't merit national attention or wouldn't be of particular interest to their audiences. But those same audiences voted with their tweets, giving the story the social proof it needed to be escalated into the top-tier media dialogue and all-day, live trial coverage. This misalignment demonstrated two things with refreshing clarity. First, neither the spread of information nor the consumption of information relies on traditional media anymore. Second, while gatekeeping still exists, the media will respond with coverage if persuaded by enough social proof.

Media gatekeepers are now able to control the flow of their information only through their owned properties. Other stories, narratives, and characters have an unprecedented ability to compete with the traditional players, and, increasingly, they're able to win. One story that's particularly hard to bury: the data isn't looking good for traditional media. Ad revenue for national newspapers is declining by double digits year over year.[19] Television consumption by the coveted 18-to 24-year-old segment is waning.[20] Publishing, too, is undergoing a rapid transformation. E-book sales are beating out every other format in book sales for the first time.[21] Amazon founder Jeff Bezos has shared that e-books "is a multibillion-dollar category for us and growing fast," while physical book sales are experiencing record-low growth rates.[22] Both booksellers and publishers have had little choice but to embrace the trend, but for ailing retailers like Barnes and Noble, it may be too little, too late. Author Clay Shirky told me:

> Publishers are a little bit mystified that although none of their mechanisms for calling attention to things have gotten worse, by comparison the public's ability to call attention to things has gotten immeasurably much better. Whereas the public writ large, when they decide they like something, whether it's a LOLcat or anything else, it can blow up.

The War for Impressions

Competition between media firms of every type now hinges, more than ever before, on speed and volume. Being the first on the story means more impressions, views, and ultimately advertising dollars. Similarly, having more content to fill the airwaves in a 24-hour news cycle, or new articles to greet visitors when they visit your home page, is an advantage over the competition in the contest for the increasingly fleeting attention span of the modern consumer. Gawker Media, the empire behind hugely successful blogs like *Gawker* (gossip), *Kotaku* (gaming), and *Gizmodo* (gadgets), makes no bones about it, which ruffles more than a few old-guard feathers. In an interview on NBC's *Rock Center,* Gawker Media CEO Nick Denton was almost shockingly straightforward about it:

> *People need to get their head around the fact that the web is different, that we publish faster, we change faster, we correct faster, and frankly, that our standards of publication are lower.*[23]

Gawker has a public leaderboard where writers are ranked based on new visitors and page views for their pieces across all the company's owned media properties, and a large television in the newsroom displays and updates the board in real time to stir up competition among the writers.

The practice isn't isolated to start-up type media operations either, reports the Gray Lady herself, the *New York Times:*

> *Tracking how many people view articles, and then rewarding—or shaming—writers based on those results has become increasingly common in old and new media newsrooms. The* Christian Science Monitor *now sends a daily e-mail message to its staff that lists the number of page views for each article on the paper's Web site that day. [. . .] The* New York Times, *the* Washington Post *and the* Los Angeles Times *all display a 'most viewed' list on their home pages. Some media outlets, including Bloomberg News and Gawker Media, now pay writers based in part on how many readers click on their articles.*[24]

The New Content Creators

Even nonmedia companies are getting into this game, realizing that great, shareable content delivered at high velocity can increase brand loyalty, awareness, and sales. *iQ*, an interactive magazine of sorts from Intel, uses algorithmic and employee curation of articles from around the web to "Share and source content that inspires, educates, entertains and helps all of us to better understand our modern world."[25] Energy drink Red Bull has an entire spin-off enterprise devoted to publishing, including *The Red Bulletin*, a glossy lifestyle magazine made the old-fashioned way—with paper. But most brands are having trouble keeping up with the need to provide fresh content at an ever-increasing rate. One study of 1,000 business-to-business marketers revealed that 41 percent of them consider the production of engaging content their "biggest content marketing challenge," followed by "producing enough content" at 20 percent.[26] Companies across the spectra of size and type, including GE, Cisco, Boeing, and Dogfish Head Beer, are hiring trained journalists and editors to create the kind of compelling content that marketers often struggle with. Seizing on this new trend, Contently and a handful of other start-ups have emerged to help brands find freelance journalists.

You Are a Source

This explosion in demand for content is a massive opportunity for people looking to build audiences and credibility in their respective fields. No matter what your area of expertise, there are people today, with established platforms, looking for sources and contributors just like you. The more visible you are online, the likelier you'll be approached to provide a quote, a comment, or even a full op-ed. In its "Digital Journalism Study," PR group Oriella found that reporters are becoming exceptionally reliant on new media for sources. The study determined that:

- 54 percent of journalists now use "microblogging updates" (e.g., posts from Twitter, Facebook, and other international networks), and 44 percent use blogs to source information from individuals and accounts they are already familiar with
- 26 percent of respondents use "unfamiliar social media sources" in the same way
- 69 percent of journalists in the United States maintain a personal blog, which is the perfect initial social media side door for aspiring sources

Slipping Standards

There's a bit of a dark side here. When things are mass-produced, quality tends to suffer, and the things themselves are cheapened. Content is being affected by the same forces that were at play in the Industrial Revolution and are at play now in globalization. Scale cuts corners, glosses over flaws, and overindexes on quantity—on getting it out the door. Standards are easier to maintain when the competition maintains them, too, but what if you're a century-old newspaper and your competition is the *Gawkers* of the world? Good luck telling investors that your newsroom won't participate in the click contests that shape and define modern media. In this landscape, those who understand the game have the power and the floor.

Warhol's 15 minutes of fame has been cut down to 15 seconds, or however long it takes to get bumped to page two. Platforms are no longer built brick by brick and dollar by dollar. Sometimes they are flash floods of attention; most of the time they ebb and flow like calmer waters. But they are always moving, never still. There's no resting anymore on that single mention in the *Wall Street Journal* or *TechCrunch*. Eyes on the horizon, always—opportunities are everywhere, but so is your competition. It doesn't matter that you're a better source. It doesn't matter that you don't share a common customer base. The competition is vying for the attention of the blogger or journalist who competes for impressions with his or her colleagues, rival outlets, and pictures of puppies in adorable costumes.

Visible and Accessible

Just one link in a well-trafficked article can drive thousands of new visitors to your site and result in dozens of new blog subscribers while taking your search engine visibility to new highs. Your words in a top-tier publication serve as convincing evidence of your command of a subject; this can beef up your bio and portfolio while opening up many more opportunities with writers from other outlets filing derivative stories or bookmarking your profile for future outreach. Opportunities like this build on one another. If you become known as a good source, your name will be shared with others, and you'll be approached by some of the same writers over and over again. Through just one person who I met at a conference and kept in touch with across social channels, I've contributed to half a dozen articles on high-profile sites like *FastCompany.com*, and I now have familiarity with and access to the editors of those sites when I want to contribute my own bylines.

The key is being proactive and not expecting people to come to you. If you want to become a known quantity, you have to get in front of people. Engage through social media with platform gate-keepers; comment on and share their work. Contribute in small ways here and there with added perspective or constructive criticism. Link to their pieces from your own blog. Ask them if they accept guest posts, and send them original work. What you'll soon realize is that a lot of bloggers and editors see good guest posts as a "day off," one less post they have to worry about writing themselves. Knowing this, you should always frame your outreach in terms of an opportunity for *them*, not a request from *you*. And if you drive traffic and sharing, you'll be invited back. It's like a comedy club:

if you draw a crowd and the members of the audience buy a lot of drinks, you'll get stage time whenever you want.

Everyone's a Critic

This all means that the cost of entry into the media landscape for the average person has fallen dramatically. Want to be a singer? Post videos on YouTube and record your own MP3s. Want to be a writer? Start blogging and put together an e-book. Want to be a critic? Start critiquing the films you see and post them online. You'll encounter very few filters along the way.

But there's another side of gatekeeping that benefits those who are let through. Gatekeepers have audiences and resources. Once you're through, you're in front of a crowd that has been gathered *for* you, not *by* you. Gatekeepers have promotional budgets, ratings, and sales targets to hit and bosses to please. Letting you through is an investment. They might buy ads for you or give you airtime or book you high-profile gigs—expensive, time-consuming things that are extremely difficult for the average person to achieve alone.

When you're on your own, building an audience is the hardest part. There's a saying that drives me nuts: "Content is king." Oh that it were so! What about the millions of great authors, musicians, and comedians you've never heard of, and never will? Their content is superb, and yet they toil in relative obscurity. Why? They devote most or all of their time to perfecting the content and not enough time building an audience for it.

The Embassy of You: Better Your Life by Blogging

This section isn't called "How to Get Blog Comments" or "How to Make Your Posts Go Viral." Google those things if you'd like, but be wary of what you read. When the how-to format meets blogging, the quality of advice often gets iffy. Blog comments, "engagement," subscribers, top 100 placement—they're all means to an ill-defined end. These things are not the goal; they're only loose indicators that you're on track toward something bigger. Everyone blogs to better his or her life in some way. Blogging can make a very real impact on that one big goal, if you stay away from measuring your success in ways that have nothing to do with what you're really after.

To make an impact, you need a central outpost that acts as the heart of your social media presence. Blogs are great for this. They are built for long-form content like blog posts, but they can also be a great way to aggregate your tweets and YouTube videos and link to your Facebook and LinkedIn profiles and other digital footprints you'd like to showcase. Think of your blog as an embassy. If strangers were to visit the Embassy of You, what would you want them to see? More importantly, what would *they* want to see?

Play to your strengths and write about what you know. If you're trying to prove to the world that you're an expert in something, abide by the old writers' saying, "Show, don't tell." Don't simply *tell* people about your expertise. Anyone can do that. You need to *show* it. Write with authority about something you have passion for, and your "expert self" will steal the show. Most of the people you're competing with will start by talking about themselves, playing up their status, telling the world how great they are at something—and little else.

Define your niche. Generalists usually don't get very far, because they're going toe-to-toe with millions of others who have been doing it longer and probably better. Google likes niches, too. Unique content fares better in search results, so ask yourself what the people you'd like to influence are searching for.

Don't be shy about featuring what others have said about you and your work. On the page of your blog that explains who you are, let others tell the story for you—they're better at it. Pretend it's the back of a book. Public praise by a third party is infinitely more effective than self-congratulatory copy. Successful blogger Brian Clark put it this way: "What other people say about you is more important than what you say about yourself."[27]

Some of the praise you feature will come naturally, even unexpectedly. But you'll usually need to ask for it when you've done good work, so make a habit of it. Be sure to disclose that you plan on putting their words on your blog. Most will be flattered.

After putting in all that work, the last thing you want to do is sit back and wait, believing content is king. The concept of reciprocity should guide your efforts to promote your blog. Think about what actions you want people to take when they visit your blog; literally make a list of them. Then make a list of bloggers who you respect, whose work you enjoy, and whom you'd like to get to know better. Make sure to include bloggers who *aren't* hugely popular yet; due to the volume of activity on their blogs (and also perhaps due to their egos), well-known bloggers are less likely to reciprocate.

Now the fun part. Take your list of people, visit their blogs, and start doing the things on your other list. Comment on their blogs; subscribe to their newsletters; send thoughtful tweets in their direction. You'll quickly find that people like people who validate their work in these ways, and they like people who share their passions. Many of them will take a moment to discover who you are by following the link in your Twitter profile or the backlink in your blog comments. And then they'll reciprocate by commenting, sharing your content, or doing something else similar to what you did for them. Just don't hold it against them if some of them don't. Reciprocation is not a right, and people that feel entitled to it usually aren't well liked.

The best part about building a network of influence that leads back to your blog—and you—is that the actions you take pay for themselves many times over even if they aren't reciprocated. If you're reading the best bloggers in your space, you're constantly learning how to do your job better. Reading great work is rewarding in and of itself. You're also gathering ideas to discuss and material to quote and to reference, and you're getting insight into what seems to be resonating with their audience, with which there is bound to be significant overlap if you're truly in a similar niche. I'll reiterate that common activity and engagement metrics shouldn't be used to validate your efforts, but they can serve as indicators of which content seems to be hitting the mark. Start experimenting with emulating some of the best of what you read, the stuff that really seems to ignite dialogue in the comments or spread like wildfire across the social web.

Emulate does not mean copy. In fact, the best thing you can do as an emerging blogger is give proper credit where it is due. Even if a post is only loosely based on another's idea, be sure to acknowledge this by letting your readers know and linking to the original. This isn't just a goodwill exercise and the right thing to do; it's a strategic must. Most bloggers receive "pingback" alerts, which tell them when someone has linked to one of their posts or pages and where the link lives online. They'll often follow the pingback trail to your blog, which can be the beginning or acceleration of a rewarding relationship. It's a special thrill to learn that someone you truly admire has subscribed to your blog.

Finding the time to write can be difficult. I've been blogging for years, and the truth is, it doesn't get any easier—but it does get more rewarding. Once you start to see your disparate efforts coalesce into results, blogging becomes something you can't imagine not doing. One of the secrets to building awareness and influence is that almost everyone wants more content, even the biggest names in your space. Of any tactic I've pursued to build social access and influence through blogging, guest posts are the most effective. The value created by a good guest post on someone else's blog is pretty remarkable. Think about it: You get access to a new, larger audience. They get free content that drives traffic to their doorstep. But guest blogging is about relationships, and quality of content trails a distant second. Aspiring guest bloggers should be very familiar with the style and subject matter of the host blog. They should cultivate a rapport with the blogger by leaving interesting comments on the blog posts, sharing their work, and making themselves known. This is also a way for the host blogger to become familiar with the guest blogger's writing style and area expertise. You're ready, as a guest blogger, when you can be reasonably sure the host blogger will recognize your name in the "from" line of an e-mail and when you have an idea that will fit right in with the blog's content. Don't make the mistake of reaching out without something specific in mind. And if the host blogger shows interest in the content you propose, don't waste an opportunity to get the terms right for your guest post. Make sure to discuss how your bio and byline will appear, where it will link to (a social profile, your blog, or both), and whether or not you'll be able to cross-post it to your blog with a link back to the original. Most top bloggers are flexible on these items and happy to discuss them, as long as you give them clear input and don't nitpick.

The mere fact that you are blogging means that you are positively differentiating yourself from the pack. Everyone wants 50 comments on every post, 10,000 subscribers, and a healthy dose of ad revenue. But the truth is, only a tiny percentage of bloggers experience any of that. Too many bloggers start comparing themselves with the best in the business right out of the gate. While it's great to learn from the best, it's not smart to expect the results they have from less work. It's also not smart to write your blog off as a failure because it's not getting the activity you're after, even though you are putting in the work. If it never becomes anything more than a record of your thoughts or a collection of your best work, it is still worth it—and you are still doing something valuable that most are not.

- You are a source for a story being written right now. Make your expertise visible and stay accessible.
- Your blog is the Embassy of You. It should showcase your work, knowledge, social proof, and accessibility.
- Build a network of influence that leads back to your blog. Engage with the top bloggers in your space through links, comments, and other social interactions. Pitch relevant guest posts once they know who you are.

CHAPTER 2

From the Outside, Looking In

One million. That's the number of job applications Google receives per year for its 6,000 annual openings, according to the *Seattle Post-Intelligencer*. Of course, anyone familiar with Google's workplace culture and legacy of innovation would expect a ratio like this. But it's not just bleeding-edge tech jobs that are generating amazing levels of interest. A Ford plant in Louisville received nearly 17,000 applicants for 1,800 new jobs, a ratio of 9.4 job seekers for every opening.[1] According to the Bureau of Labor Statistics, at the beginning of the recession, "the number of unemployed persons per job opening was 1.8," while the ratio at the official end of the recession (June 2009) had risen to "6.1 unemployed persons per job opening."[2] The number of doors is growing at a much slower rate than the number of people trying to pass through them.

A Rat Race to the Starting Line

Capitalism's culture of competition has served many of us well. Free markets have the capacity to create great wealth and power for those willing and able to fight for it, and you'll find this competitive instinct in almost all independently successful people. It's a trait that is endlessly romanticized and hard not to admire. But instincts are blind. They tell us to take on a lot of challenges we're better off avoiding. In particular, they cloud our judgment in two critical areas—probability and opportunity cost. Probability is simple. Ideally, we'll consider the odds of our intended outcome occurring, weighing things like our true abilities, context, and timing. Based on this analysis, we decide whether we have a good shot at whatever we're after. But our competitive mindsets—and the culture we're a part of—tell us that we should stop thinking and start doing, that we can do anything we set out to do. We can't. And even if we could, we haven't considered the opportunity cost.

Opportunity cost is the value we give up when we make a particular choice over another possible choice. That value can often be measured in terms of time and money. So if our goal is to become a millionaire, we could get there by going to a top business school, working at a top company, and spending years moving up the hierarchy until we hit that magic combination of salary, bonuses, and options at the million dollar mark. But could we have done it more efficiently, more quickly, less painfully? It's hard to say when our celebrated competitive spirit makes it easy to not make the right calculations that can guide us to alternative avenues to the same (or greater) success.

One thing we're all competing for is attention. No man is an island, and no one is truly, completely, self-made. At the most basic level, we need people to give us their attention so we can make our pitch. We need to earn audiences, and usually those audiences lie beyond purposely built barriers that are designed to keep everyone but the chosen few out. We keep throwing ourselves against this front door, hoping it will eventually give. Sometimes it does—but was it worth it? Shouldn't we have been looking for the side door instead?

It reminds me of a few concerts I've been to. Platinum pass holders are let in first, in the order they arrive. Regular pass holders are let in *only after* enough platinum pass holders have entered, and then they are let in one by one, in the order they arrived. Any platinum pass holders who show up late can get in before all the remaining regular pass holders. In this example, whom are we competing against? We might think we're competing against every other attendee, but we're not. Platinum people have it made—they may jostle for position with each other, but they'll get a great seat, guaranteed. Regular people are really competing against one another for the extremely limited access that the platinum people have no need for.

Open doors create inefficiency. Each person who walks through them requires attention in some form or another, a resource that's easily exhausted. Lines are formed. Credentials are screened more closely. Contact information is pulled from websites. Access is constricted and streamlined to make sure that people, requests, and time are managed in a way that prevents total meltdown. People understand this intuitively—when they all want something finite, they can't all get it. But they still want it.

The world relies on gatekeepers even more heavily during times of uncertainty and crisis. When more people are calling in favors, digging deeper into their contacts, and seeking the kinds of jobs they once balked at, the front door is reinforced to compensate. Shutting others out isn't something people enjoy doing, but something they believe they must do—a duty. Front doors are narrowed and shut especially tight in light of facts like this one: the 12,511,000 recession-era college graduates in the United States are doing everything they can to walk through them, and they can't all fit. Eighty-three applicants for every graduate-level opening in the United Kingdom[3] means that companies are forced to reevaluate every aspect of their hiring practices, down to the paper their rejection notices are printed on.

Success requires more and more gatekeeping to keep systems humming. A small business doesn't need a call center to service customers; the call center is the agitating by-product of a company's successful scaling to a point where access needs to be limited or diverted to allow other areas of the business to operate without distraction. Similarly, actors who haven't yet "made it" are eager for inquiries and make sure their direct contact information is found easily. Working actors, however, divert inquiries to publicists and agents, whose job, in part, is to guard access to their clients. You may be able to get a meeting with your county commissioner, but very few can get one with the governor. And it's easy to forget that this is generally a good thing— we want people who have the capacity to make big decisions to be able to focus; we don't want the nut who ruins every town hall meeting to have weekly one-on-ones with Mark Zuckerberg.

Fortunate Sons (and Daughters)

Every time a great position opens up at a respected company, a familiar sequence of events is set in motion. First, the company will probably try to fill the position internally. This is much more efficient and much less costly than recruiting outsiders. Even the most experienced external applicant doesn't stand a chance against the less-experienced internal applicant who has delivered for the company in the past. Then, professional networks are tapped, and "people who know people" in the company are brought in. If they know the *right* people, they will likely be hired even if they're really not all that qualified relative to the average external candidate. Odds are, the position will be filled at this point before the outside world hears word one about it. If for some reason the position remains unfilled, outside applicants are finally allowed to compete. And they go for it, because they don't know there's a better way to play. It's true; the more they put into getting this job through traditional means, the greater their chances of getting it—but those chances are still pretty pathetic. They're spending less time developing alternative means of access to hiring managers. Less time looking for other desirable openings they're better equipped to compete for. Less time building relationships that will help them immensely if they're patient enough to cultivate them.

Michael David Wuest's story is a lot like my own. In 2008, his college internship was about to run its course, and he wasn't getting any traction finding a job to transition into after graduation. It's all too familiar:

> *I spent about 50 hours tweaking my résumé to make it perfect,*
> *but was having zero luck getting any call backs or interviews from*
> *the hundreds of emails and applications I had filled out. Nobody*
> *wanted to hire a young MBA with very limited experience, espe-*
> *cially in the middle of 2008. Quite the stressful time in my life.*

But then Michael found a side door in the form of *One Day One Job*, a blog that was conducting a "social experiment" by providing Facebook advertising credits for people to market themselves to employers. He aimed his ad at Sprint and paid $5 worth of credits for 32 clicks. Five Sprint employees e-mailed him, and he landed a phone interview—right before Sprint underwent a hiring freeze. But Michael's escapades attracted the attention of a food service company seeking a marketing manager, and he found his next job.

Influence Is Earned (and Learned)

I had never heard of my supposedly "influential" copanelist. We were talking to MBA candidates about successful social media strategies for business. He had around 100,000 Twitter followers, which made my modest following in the low five digits seem insignificant. I had done a little digging on this person, finding his name pop up here and there on SEO (search engine optimization) forums—but curiously, never on social media blogs. Stranger still, he rarely ever tweeted. And yet the aspects of his online persona that he could control, like his Twitter bio and Facebook page, claimed deep experience and extensive knowledge in social media. In the green room before the event, we chatted for a few minutes. Like me, he lived in Austin, so naturally I asked him if he attended some of the educational and networking groups that had helped me build my own influence locally, such as Social Media Club Austin. "No," he told me, "Not really." This was curious, but not *that* strange; participation in these groups was not a necessary stop in the path to influence. I tried to establish mutual contacts. Did he know Simon Salt and Kat Mandelstein, local thought leaders who excelled at connecting people and helping those around them build notoriety? He was evasive, offering only that he thought they had "crossed paths." The panel began, and while I tried to draw on my working experience, he seemed only to copy and paste from his days as an SEO guru, adapting his points ever so slightly, but not so convincingly, to the social media context. I could tell my answers were resonating with the crowd and his were falling short. When the questions started, I received the bulk of them. That night, I asked a few of the most well-connected people I knew if they had ever heard of this man, whose Twitter following dwarfed that of anyone I knew. None of them had. We later concluded that he had acquired his following by applying some less than savory techniques that had everything to do with exploiting loopholes and nothing to do with earning influence. I wondered, when he tweeted, how many of those 100,000 followers paid any attention. Theoretically, he could access any of them at any time, but it was clear to me that this access had little value, since it carried with it no influence.

Access is meaningless without influence. What will we do once we've gained access to effect the outcomes we desire? If we don't know or if we make the wrong choices after access, we risk losing everything we've worked for. It's a question to ask long before being let in. Equally important is the fact that influence can be used to unlock doors we've finally reached, like Ali Baba's magic words, "open sesame," at the mouth of the cave of treasures. Influence helps us get there, and it allows us to get things done when we've arrived.

Social media can be used to cultivate influence more easily than ever before. Gone are the days when only published authors and industry leaders could generate media coverage. It's no longer necessary to know a company decision maker to be seriously considered as a vendor—or job candidate. Using our social content (tweets, blog posts, etc.) to establish expertise shows the people we want to influence that we know what we're talking about. Our following and the activity we generate along the way, as our ideas spread and our networks grow, show them that other people are listening to us and that many are like them. Tweets are taking the place of long-form testimonials and references; and follower count, blog subscribers, and Klout scores are being used—often mistakenly—as a proxy for the amount of cachet one has earned.

All this has a powerful democratizing effect on the accumulation and distribution of influence. Influence is no longer reserved for the elite or for the longtime insider. The scope of the people we trust to inform our views and our decisions is massively wider than it once was, for both consumers and businesses. Companies are using crowdsourcing and direct consumer feedback to design their next product lines. People are getting their news from nontraditional outlets like *Gawker*, *Slate*, and *Salon*. We're ditching our cable boxes for the universe of content the web offers us instantly.

This democratization of influence has led to a diffusion of power, and the number of entities we're competing against for influence has grown just as fast as the social web. The playing field between the average person and traditional media outlets may be leveling, but more and more players are entering the stadium every day. I spoke to one of those players, John Dumas, who has made a career out of interviewing well-known entrepreneurs like Seth Godin and Guy Kawasaki on his *EntrepreneurOnFire* podcast. He first works to build name recognition in the mind of the prospective interviewee:

By adding good content and comments over a period of time, one can become a valued member of any community, so when the request is posed, it is coming from a community member, not an unknown email, and the results are fantastic.

When Dumas records a particularly good podcast with a guest who nonlisteners will recognize, he moves quickly to expand his audience through a mix of paid and earned promotion:

I interviewed Seth Godin and decided to try this whole "promoted posts" thing on Facebook. That one post went viral and received hundreds and hundreds of likes, shares and comments. It exposed my brand to a whole new segment of the Facebook population, and was an eye opener to me as to the power of great content.

King Without a Crowd?

One of the biggest mistakes in influence generation stems from the truism, "Content is king." As I asked in Chapter 1, if content is king, why do so many great blogs go unread? Why do some of the cleverest tweets come from people with tiny followings? Because content needs a constantly growing delivery network to spread and reach the people we want to influence. Expertise needs an audience if it's ever to be converted into influence.

As my friend Brian Solis has written, the *true* king is context, not content.[4] Spend too much time crafting content and not enough time architecting the context in which it can thrive—your network—and your influence will stagnate. Find the right balance, and your influence will soar.

One's social footprint can certainly inhibit success, and employers are turning to social background checks to dig up inappropriate behavior when screening applicants. But more and more, just having a large and influential social footprint can open doors, and not just in job seeking. Event promoters are now offering exclusive VIP admission—even full-ride travel and hotel stays—to those with enough social influence in their niche. Often these influencers are chosen based on their Klout scores, an algorithmically generated ranking that approximates one's social influence. In a comment on my blog, Klout CEO Joe Fernandez described his company's perspective: "We see our data as a way to augment or balance the 'human touch' that will always be needed to identify influencers."[5]

Valuing Influence

I had a brief skirmish over a Twitter account with a previous employer. Even though I intended to use the account primarily for personal use, I chose to combine my first name with the name of my employer in my Twitter handle—a poor decision in retrospect. Over time, I built a small but active following of friends, clients, prospects, and industry experts. The modest success it had generated turned out to be a blessing and a curse, because every time it helped close a new sale, the management's desire to keep it with the company grew stronger. Although my departure from the company was amicable enough, one of the first things we discussed when I gave notice was ownership of that account. The company demanded that I hand over complete access, but I wanted to think about it. I stepped out to get coffee, and when I returned, my work computer had been "reclaimed," and the Twitter account had a new password. I was upset, but not prepared for a battle—it was one of my first jobs out of college, and I needed references (or so I thought). The strange ordeal proved to me that social influence wasn't some coveted status one suddenly achieves, but a persistent and evolving attribute of *any* social media presence.

And keep in mind that not everyone is treated as I was. Jim Roberts was an assistant managing editor at the *New York Times*. He left in January 2012 with his 75,000 followers intact, presumably without a fight. Roberts's following is the equivalent of roughly 1 percent of the 7.3 million followers of @nytimes. A *Times* spokesperson said that while there is no "specific policy in place that covers this kind of situation," Roberts's "followers are his and will choose to continue to follow him [which I suspect to be the case], or not."[6]

Implicitly or explicitly, influencers are being regaled with gifts and access for one reason above all others. Brands are hoping they will use their influence to spread positive word of mouth about their products and services. Social influence is now monetizable, exchangeable for what we're really after. This is a power that we're only beginning to realize we possess. Employers are already starting to ask applicants for their Twitter follower counts, and some job seekers are actually being screened out for not having "enough."[7] Our social footprints are now our books of business and are soon to be taken as seriously.

Be Three-Dimensional

I used to sell mobile apps and custom blogs to real estate agents. Unlike most decision makers, their livelihood depended on having their direct contact information findable. Even getting in touch with the head broker of a 300-agent firm was easy; all of the agents' cell numbers were right there on their websites. Lucky me, I thought. But when I called them, they'd give me short shrift. Many would hang up within seconds. I was competing for their attention against a sea of other salespeople, all of us vying for their attention in *the same exact way*. No matter how incredible my offer was, it wouldn't be considered because they didn't know me (or my company) from Adam, and I was one of 5 to 10 faceless salespeople who had called them that day already.

Anyone in sales or marketing can relate to this problem. The solution? Use social media to make yourself "three-dimensional" and open up a side door of access.

People like to do business—at any scale—with people they know, like, and trust. Cold calling and e-mail blasts are numbers games with long odds. By creating a compelling social media presence, you're humanizing yourself, establishing your expertise, and engaging in a way that differentiates you from just another strange voice on the end of a phone call—you're making yourself three-dimensional in the mind of the prospect. In my case, I started joining real estate marketing Twitter chats, building my Facebook and Twitter networks by posting interesting content, and blogging about solutions to some of the industry pain points I was hearing about. When I started calling again, I was no longer the anonymous sales guy. I was the guy who taught them that cool Twitter search trick, or the guy whose blog they had subscribed to. I had earned their attention and became the obvious choice whenever they needed something I was selling.

Kathy Le Backes rents out "mismatched vintage place settings" through her business, The Vintage Table Co. She told me about some of the tactics she has successfully used to find new clients. One of her biggest victories started with a simple tweet to a dinner party service she had read about: "love your business! let me know if you ever need vintage place settings for your dinners." An e-mail arrived a few days later with an invitation to connect, and she's been working with the service for the better part of a year. Her Twitter strategy is a mix of social signals, friendly conversation, and a touch of discipline. She tries to follow five businesses in related industries every day (including wedding planners, caterers, bakers, and stylists), and she has noticed that small businesses tend to follow back shortly after receiving Twitter's "new follower" e-mails. "Taking advantage of the conversational nature of Twitter, I would interact with them" by asking questions and complimenting their work. "People love that attention. As a result, they started paying more attention to my work. Interacting with me more. I can't tell you how many times this strategy has resulted in face-to-face meetings (kind of like online dating!)," which have "resulted in client referrals, collaborations and longstanding relationships." Soon, the network effect kicked in, and

Le Backes found herself getting business from followers of followers: "One of the most sought-after celebrity wedding planners hired me for Jessica Simpson's baby shower. When I asked her how she found me, she said, 'Twitter.'"

Enrich the Exchange

Like anyone else with any control over vendor selection, I get a lot of phone and e-mail pitches. And like anyone else who values his time (and sanity), I screen most of them out. The pitches that I do pay attention to are different. They're from people who have first taken a look at my social footprint, and that of my company, to equip themselves for a personalized approach and higher-level conversation. Often they'll interact with me via social media first to establish a rapport—they'll comment on my blog posts or retweet a few of my updates. They'll also use social media to enrich the standard phone and e-mail exchanges, starting out by telling me their thoughts on my newest blog post or by sending me one-off, non-"salesy" e-mails sharing something they read that will likely interest me, too. These techniques work because they simultaneously help personalize the approach and build substantive relationships—two things that have always been extremely important to successful sales and marketing efforts and that are easier to do than ever before thanks to social media. So why don't we see them more often?

Rules from Another Era

The rules and etiquette of access were written by Those Who Cannot Be Accessed, the tiny minority who has no problem getting through the front door. Once in, they're asked to shut the door behind them, and they do. After that, an open front door is just a distraction from the important things they're doing.

Those Who Cannot Be Accessed will always be let in. For others the door will never open, but most of them will still line up in case it does. Almost all of us are "others," or we started out that way. We still play by the rules of access, not because we're stupid or because we lack creativity, but because they're the only rules we know—and because the people we want to engage with have told us that if the rules are followed, we may just get what we want. We'll keep working on our cover letters, leaving messages, and smiling and dialing until then.

Here's the secret: the rules haven't been updated in a long time. They tell us nothing about social media, and social media side doors are being created every single day for those who know this.

Faith McKinney is a full-time janitor at an Indianapolis post office, but Faith's access to A-list personalities is extraordinary. She has interviewed Dan Rather, Tavis Smiley, and other household names for a local online magazine. Faith's *method* is old-fashioned, but her *tools* are modern: whenever she finds out that celebrities will visit her hometown, she contacts them via social media for an interview. "The answer," she says, "is almost always yes." She has been able to leverage her success into a motivational speaking sideline, and she's on her way to her goal of "traveling the world with [her] family while earning a great living."

Welcome to Lexington

The ad agency business is arguably more of a "whom you know" game than any other. The big-name accounts that upstarts need to make a ripple tend to prefer safety and repeatability over creativity, and the big agencies are long on the former and typically short on the latter. Getting in the front door of a household name like A&W Restaurants would be extremely difficult for a small outfit like Cornett Integrated Marketing Solutions, out of Lexington, Kentucky. "No one at the agency actually knew anyone at A&W,"

according to *Mashable*.[8] "No one knew if the company was looking for a new ad agency." That didn't stop Cornett from blowing open a side door using a LinkedIn bomb:

> *In April, everyone in the agency sent LinkedIn requests to A&W Restaurants President Kevin Bazner and Director of Marketing Sarah Blasi at the exact same time. The messages were all headed "Welcome to Lexington" because A&W had just moved its head-quarters from Louisville after being spun off from Yum Brands.*
>
> *Blasi says she was at a photo shoot and "all of the sudden I got about 35 LinkedIn notifications at once." At first she thought some-one had hacked her account. Then she read them. "They were all individual stories about their personal relationships with A&W Restaurants." One was from a guy who visited the restaurant with his grandfather when he was a kid. Another was from someone whose first date with the woman who became his wife was at an A&W.*

It worked. Cornett is now A&W's lead agency, which will undoubt-edly attract other large clients.

If a CEO Blogs, and No One Comments

Thomson Reuters is constantly hiring, with more than a thousand openings advertised on its website at any given time. The average post on Reuters CEO Tom Glocer's personal blog receives about six comments, and many posts have no comments whatsoever.[9] It's likely that Tom Glocer reads every comment, because he replies on occasion. This is the CEO of a company with 55,000 employees and over $10 billion in annual revenue. He doesn't tweet often, but he does reply to some of the mentions he gets (about 20 per month). Most posts on *The Knowledge Effect*, an official Thomson Reuters blog, have no comments. @JobsWithUs, the official Thomson Reuters recruiting account, is rarely mentioned by job seekers. Something isn't adding up. Where are the job seekers? Where are the vendors who want some of that $10 billion spent on them?

Saatchi & Saatchi is synonymous with innovation in the agency space. The company is absurdly successful and lists "6 of the top 10 and over half of the top 50 global advertisers" as clients.[10] It's on your top 10 list if you're a recent graduate or agency job seeker; it's the agency you want to partner with if you're in business development; it's the agency you want to sell to if you sell or market to agencies. Here's what Michelle Greenhalgh, a client partner of graduate recruitment at the firm, wrote in the *Guardian*:

> *Recently I have been feted by flowers, cupcakes, customised Monopoly board games, cold hard cash, cocktail making kits (complete with fresh limes and tequila), cuddly toys, bricks and a life-size human cardboard cut-out. These have all been sent to me in a bid by people wanting to get my attention, and stand out in the quest for work experience or a job at Saatchi & Saatchi.[11]*

It's not that aspiring Saatchi employees don't attempt to find social media side doors. Each month, one or two hopefuls post to the flagship Saatchi Facebook page, like this young Londoner, who writes, "Subliminal message> hiremehiremehiremehireme." No response from Saatchi, or anyone else. A graphic design student tweets a cute holiday greeting video her classmates made to @saatchi_sisomo. Nothing. Some, like Steven Severn, have gotten more creative. Severn decided to use targeted Facebook ads to pursue Saatchi LA. Clicks went to his LinkedIn profile, and "after two weeks and only spending $3.43, employees of Saatchi & Saatchi LA began sending me messages through LinkedIn praising me for my efforts and were more than willing to help me land my dream job."[12]

Standing out is especially important in creative industries, but it doesn't always take a stunt (or "cold hard cash"). Like Tom Glocer at Thomson Reuters, Saatchi's legendary CEO, Kevin Roberts, has his own blog.[13] It's a ghost town that rarely sees more than one comment per post. Where are the Saatchi hopefuls? We can't know whether or not a single, well-written comment would change anything for a Saatchi job seeker, but we do know that Kevin Roberts would at least read it: "All comments must be approved by the blog author." And how many Saatchi & Saatchi job seekers get to interact with Kevin Roberts at *any* stage in the hiring process? How many salespeople or marketers get to speak directly to the CEO of one of the top agencies in the world?

What would you do for the chance to ask Warren Buffett anything? According to the *Wall Street Journal*,[14] "There are few prizes more coveted than the opportunity to ask Warren Buffett a question at Berkshire Hathaway's annual shareholders meeting." The notoriously inaccessible titan answers 20 to 30 audience questions every year, and the rules have been changed several times in favor of more equitable question selection. Most recently, raffles were set up in multiple locations throughout the meeting venue, and Fidelity Investments saw this for what it was—an open side door. Although the company "holds about $4 billion of Berkshire shares, or a roughly 2% stake in the company," this equity alone still isn't enough for an audience with Buffett. Fidelity had 40 of its analysts enter several raffles each, netting this 2 percent stakeholder a whopping 20 percent of all the audience questions asked. Other attendees found their own side doors. Both managing partners of investing house T2 Partners were able to ask Buffett questions this year, after they spotted an overflow room in which the raffle wasn't attracting many entries. Although neither of these side doors involved social media, their discovery and *usage* reflect exactly the kind of thinking required to uncover access opportunities in the social space. If only Buffett tweeted more!

Even Giants Use Side Doors

Even companies like Salesforce.com, a behemoth in customer relationship management, get snubbed from time to time. What started as a behind-the-scenes conflict between two billionaire founders and their companies spilled into the public eye with a tweet from Salesforce.com CEO Marc Benioff, in which he accused Oracle CEO Larry Ellison of canceling Benioff's keynote at an Oracle conference. As a result, Benioff invited conference-goers to a nearby restaurant to hear him speak. The invitation spread like wildfire across Twitter. With the aid of the provocative hashtags #bannedkeynote and #guerillakeynote, the venue reached capacity quickly. "Protesters" were seen on street corners, carrying signs emblazoned with slogans suggesting that Benioff was "too innovative" for the OpenWorld conference.[15] His tweets whipped bloggers and Twitter influencers into a frenzy of pro-Salesforce coverage and speculation, and the company leveraged its social presence to drive viewers to photos and a live video stream of the mock protests and Benioff's talk.[16] That day, Google and Facebook ads began popping up with faux revolutionary calls to action like, "You Can Cancel Our Keynote but You Can't Stop the Cloud. Watch Marc's #guerillakeynote!"

The Cloud Must Go On!

You Can Cancel Our Keynote but You Can't Stop the Cloud. Watch Marc's #guerillakeynote!

Why We Wait

The truth is simple. Standing in line at the front door works just often enough that we keep doing it. It doesn't matter if it has never worked for *us*; we've seen it work for enough people that we believe it will for us, eventually. Our culture is saturated with front-door thinking. From backbreaking SAT prep to soul-crushing internships to the thousands of books found under "résumé writing" on Amazon .com, we are raised from an early age to believe in the front door as the *only* gateway to the realization of our ambitions.

We work tirelessly on the things that open the front door just a bit wider—we revise our résumés over and over, give the cold-call roulette another spin, buy yet another e-mail list. We're so busy practicing our "line dance" at the front door, we hardly notice when people break rank and walk around the corner. Sometimes we may even pity them for this—they've given up, quit, lost hope. But if we just peek around that corner ourselves, we'll see them opening the social media side door and walking right in.

Sunk Costs (and Other Lame Excuses)

The sunk costs fallacy is also called the Concorde fallacy, after the Concorde aircraft that was built jointly by the British and French. Long after it was clear that continued development of the plane was economically unsound, both governments continued to pursue it for fear of "wasting" the funds they had already spent on it.[17] Sunk costs have a particularly powerful effect on our ability to make good choices. We tend to value what we've put into an effort over what we stand to gain if we abandon that effort, because we are "loss averse."

Most of us—myself included—have invested thousands of hours waiting for the front door to open for us. We've worked incredibly hard on the things that are supposed to open it. At a certain point, we start to think of all the resources we've poured into a better place in line as sunk costs. Sunk costs (and perhaps cheap whiskey) are responsible for the worst decision making on the planet, the kind of thinking that perpetuated the cursed Concorde project. "You've come this far; it will all start to pay off soon," we've all told ourselves a million times. And this gives us a little endorphin boost of false hope that makes it easier to keep waiting.

The Seed of Doubt

Somewhere, locked away in a place we'd rather not visit, is the seed of doubt. As it grows, you confront uncomfortable notions: Is this the right line? The right door? Am I wasting my time?

We can, in fact, choose not to compete for a place in line. Choosing to achieve the same thing in a better, faster way is not quitting—it's winning, and it feels infinitely better than finally getting to the front of the line.

Any decision carries risks. But there's really no reason to fear "giving up" your place in line. It's not always an all-or-nothing gamble. No need for burned bridges or messy exits. Think of it as an iterative process. In version 1, you might spend half your time pursuing alternative methods of access and influence and the other half on more traditional methods. Depending on the results you see, version 2 may bump up the alternative methods to 75 percent and minimize the traditional methods to 25 percent, and so on for version 3. You'll eventually hit a tipping point at which the results from social media side-door seeking completely outshine the few results seen from front-door methods. That's when you jump in all the way. At that point, any time spent working the line at the front door to no avail will truly seem like time you could be spending finding the social media side door, making things happen. It will be the easiest opportunity cost calculation you've ever made, the one you'll kick yourself for not making years ago: boredom, idling, passivity, the familiar sting of being turned down at the gate, versus creativity, rich human interactions, and finally—finally—the kind of results you had stopped believing were possible.

Build a Better Side Door

Finding the social media side door isn't easy; there's nothing to set and forget. It requires both an insatiable appetite for knowledge and an understanding that failures can teach us just as much as wins. The moment we stop innovating is the moment we've stepped back in line for the front door, whether we realize it at the time or not. The social web is evolving at a pace that makes fools out of anyone claiming to have all the answers or to have written "the only [book or system or tool] you'll ever need." President Eisenhower might as well have been talking about social media when he said, "The world moves, and ideas that were once good are not always good."[18] You'll need to fill in the blanks for yourself, make good ideas great, and find better ways of doing things.

My first experience with social media side doors would have been far less successful had I not been able to expand on Grant Turck's experiences with Facebook ads. In fact, Turck himself learned of the idea in a job-hunting book, and I wouldn't be surprised if the authors of that book weren't themselves the originators of the idea.[19] No doubt, Turck tweaked some of their best practices to suit his unique situation, so I had the benefit of working with something that had undergone three or more layers of optimization and review before I happened upon it in his blog post. If I had been content with that and had not further customized the strategy for my own needs, I wouldn't have seen anywhere near the degree of success I ultimately enjoyed. The hundreds of people who have tried their hand at job-seeking Facebook ads after reading my account have likely seen better results more quickly than Turck and I ever did— they were the beneficiaries of yet another layer of optimization. In essence *they* learned from *my* mistakes, which is a pretty incredible deal. In private and public exchanges with these job seekers, I only ask that they return to the comments of my blog to share with other readers what did and did not work for them, what they did differently, and what other insights they think will help the next person take it even further.

Interestingly, it seems that even Facebook hadn't fully realized the potential of its ads platform for this particular goal until its employees started reading stories like mine. Facebook eventually contacted me about telling my story as part of a testimonials campaign targeting—I can only guess—job seekers (though I was happy to participate, it never materialized). As Facebook sees more and more job-seeking ads pop up on its servers, it will have a very real financial incentive to focus on innovating in this area.

Comments Build Your Brand

In early 2010, I split my time between my sales day job and my dream of writing a screenplay. My blog was just a few months old at that point. It was—and is—an interesting time to get into screenwriting, since many of our best storytellers have blogs. No need for seminars, and I wouldn't have been able to afford them anyway. Blogs were my master class. At the time, I was obsessed with the work of Robert Venditti, author of the hit graphic novels *The Surrogates* and *The Surrogates: Flesh and Bone*. Venditti had a blog, and it was pretty much devoid of comments, which baffled me. This wasn't some indie author; *The Surrogates* was being made into a Bruce Willis movie. Venditti was mainstream, his posts were excellent, and, somehow, his blog was a ghost town. Maybe, I thought, he never gets around to approving comments? So I left one, to test my theory. The mere chance that he would see it, that my comment would cross his radar, was thrilling—even if he never replied. A few days after I left my first comment (which was admittedly a bit gushing, but nonetheless heartfelt, and compared his work to that of some of the greats of the genre), Venditti sent me an e-mail. It read in part:

> *Just wanted to drop you a quick line and say thanks for the kind words about* The Surrogates *in your post comment. I'm humbled to have my book mentioned in the same sentence as the 2 you cited.*

Not a reply comment, which was the best I was hoping for, but a personal note! I was over the moon. My passion for the blog medium, because of that moment and so many others, rivals my love for screenwriting and comics.

Once I started blogging for a living at Bazaarvoice, I was eager to "comment my way through" social media side doors like the one I found with Venditti, but in a different context. In late 2010 and early 2011, I challenged myself to find work-related barriers to access and develop ways to tunnel through and around them with social media. I needed something to serve as a proof of concept of sorts—a successfully executed experiment that spoke to the value of pursuing business objectives through the simple act of commenting on blogs.

My first target was Forrester, a major technology and marketing analyst outfit with tremendous influence in web, software, and social spheres. Forrester's revenue model depends on charging for access. A typical research report can run $499 for nonmembers, and corporate memberships start in the tens of thousands for access to research and analysts. That's a pricey walled garden, but it's one that many companies simply factor into the cost of doing business. Forrester's freely accessed analyst blogs, then, seemed like a crack in the wall. First, I identified the analysts who researched and advised on our space, and there were quite a few. Too many to engage with on my own. Then I listed out factors such as how often they posted in a typical week, and I classified their responsiveness to commenters from low to high. That narrowed down the list to a handful of analysts that made sense to pursue. I commented on the first post from that group to hit my inbox, a day or two later. It was from Augie Ray, then a senior analyst focused on social media. His post had me practically drooling at the opportunity:

> I'm working on our Social Media Marketing Predictions for 2011, and for the first time on such a report, we'd like to invite the community to participate with this effort. Your ideas, feedback, criticisms and guidance will help us to do a better job of predicting the future, and anything posted here could make its way into the document published for Forrester subscribers and earn you a credit within the report.[20]

I thought for a few minutes and then contributed my comment. Augie thanked me, and two months later, a colleague forwarded me the report and asked me, "Do you know you're quoted in this?" Not only did I *not* know; I had forgotten all about the post and my comment—one of just two I had ever left in the Forrester community. The $499 report was downloaded 2,200 times, and I was thrilled to be a part of it.[21] I had found my side door, and more importantly, I had kicked off one of the most rewarding professional relationships I maintain to this day. Concept proved. Where else could I take it?

How about *Harvard Business Review*? I have always equated *HBR* with leadership. Maybe it's because I attended neither Harvard nor business school, and thus the title evokes, to me, both sources of prestige I lack. And getting column inches in *HBR* without having those two qualifications is a side door to *some* of that prestige, in much the same way that winning a radio contest for backstage passes will make you *feel* like someone cool enough to "know the band." Feelings aside, its readership is the kind of crowd you might expect to meet at Davos or Aspen Ideas: 31 percent of readers are chief officers, people like GE CEO Jeffrey Immelt. Even the *Economist* admits that *HBR* "almost single-handedly sets the management agenda."[22] Once your ink has been enshrined in its hallowed pages, you've got something in common with Jeff Bezos, Eric Schmidt, and Tony Hsieh. Suffice it to say, if you're writing for it or covered in it, your ideas are worth considering.

HBR was another "institution," like Forrester, that I wanted to leave my mark on. I read it obsessively. I submitted what I thought was my best writing ever, a piece that seeded the idea of this book, "*When Will the Social Media Gatekeepers Arrive?*" I sent it to the web editor, who governs the blog content. I'm disappointed in myself, in retrospect, for not submitting it for the print version—but barriers to access are often mental barriers that we build ourselves and dare not challenge. I never heard back from *HBR,* though I was excited when Brian Solis decided to run it.[23] The fact that *HBR* ignored what I thought was my best work made me all the more intent on breaching

HBR's walls, as if the publication were a crush brushing off my advances. High rejection rates, after all, have always been a proxy for prestige and exclusivity in the human mind.

My goals at that point were fairly modest: engage with the authors through comments on their work. One of those authors was David Armano, who had a recurring blog feature and is managing director at Edelman Digital. Everywhere I looked, I saw his ideas being discussed and adopted across the web, including in *HBR*. Just a month after I had left that fated comment on Augie's post, David added to the chorus (or cacophony) of social media predictions for 2011 with his own post.[24] His piece, unlike Augie's, was 99 percent his predictions, with a tiny call to action at the bottom: "Where do you see social media going in 2011?" I accepted the invitation, along with 91 other commenters. My comment, based on the idea that "2011 will be the year true online influencers are located," started a breakaway thread between David and me. I was pleased just to have a response from him (many of the prediction comments were met with crickets—no response at all), and as the discussion continued, it became clear that he was giving my prediction a lot of thought. I don't remember how I learned that my comment had been featured in the March 2011 print edition of *HBR*, but I remember how it felt, because I wrote about it (a tad arrogantly, in hindsight):

> *Sometimes, even those of us who "do" social media for a living become a little jaded after hearing so much unqualified talk, hyperbole and cheer-leading. It comes with the territory, I suppose. After a few big wins, it takes just a bit more to get me **really** excited. But David Armano and the* Harvard Business Review *have done exactly that, and I'm incredibly honored.*[25]

As with Augie Ray, David Armano and I went on to develop a rewarding professional relationship, the humble origins of which I'll never forget.

One of the lessons I extract from these experiences has to do with activity levels. If I had focused on establishing rapport through Twitter alone, I suspect I would have failed. Twitter as an angle of approach is deceptive because it *seems* so conversational and makes everyone appear to be naturally accessible. In a way, both of these perceptions are true, but only with a limited circle of established contacts. People on Twitter with huge followings, like Augie (16,000+) and David (57,000+), cannot be conversational with or accessible to everyone that throws a tweet or direct message (DM) their way. There aren't enough hours in the day. So they engage most often with those they already know or those they want to know that are even more influential than they are. To break into that circle—usually the only way to unlock consistent recognition and engagement—requires a less crowded entrance. Lower activity levels, more room for discussion beyond 140-character messages, fewer distractions—if you're starting to imagine a blog, you're thinking like I was thinking. When it comes to conversation, what blog posts lack in speed, they make up in depth. If Augie and David had posed the very same calls to action on Twitter, they would have been pelted with answers ranging from the asinine to the brilliant. I doubt my tweet would have made it through the storm. But on the blogs, my comments were able to compete on merit and not timing.

In the examples above, I found a way to unlock two side doors at once—the person and the institution. By finding the points where the person and the institution intersected in public, the Forrester and *HBR* blogs, respectively, I was able to access both with every comment I left. This strategy would work extremely well during a job search if the decision makers you want to reach (or their bosses) blog for the company. To illustrate one way this strategy pays off, here's what happens when anyone comments on many corporate blogs: both the author and the blog administrators get instant e-mail notifications. If that blogger is, say, the CMO, it means that the person with ultimate hiring authority in the marketing group sees it, as well as others who may weigh in on hiring decisions or have staffs of their own.

Blog comments are nothing new, and neither is their use as a means of access and influence. It was a blog comment in 2003, appropriately, that led to Matt Mullenweg's creation of WordPress, which is now the world's most popular blogging platform.[26] And a series of comments on an obscure Reddit post catapulted Des Moines resident James Erwin into fame and fortune. He left the comments in response to the question, "Could I destroy the entire Roman Empire during the reign of Augustus if I traveled back in time with a modern U.S. Marine infantry battalion or MEU [Marine Expeditionary Unit]?" According to *Wired*:

> *Within an hour, he was an online celebrity. Within three hours, a film producer had reached out to him. Within two weeks, he was offered a deal to write a movie based on his Reddit comments. Within two months, he had taken a leave from his job to become a full-time Hollywood screenwriter.*[27]

Gathering "Social Intelligence"

If you have an information advantage over the competition, you're the one who's getting through the door—or finding the undiscovered side door. Intelligence gathering with social media is an ancient art with a modern twist. Everywhere they go, people leave "social signals"—digital footprints that can tell you about their interests, desires, preferences, and a lot more. The technologies we can use to collect these signals, and isolate them from the noise, are changing all the time. But the basic principles of using social media for intelligence gathering can continue to guide us. Use these principles to craft a warm, informed approach to the person or people you want to get in front of and influence.

First, only seek out publicly available information. By this I mean nothing that is encrypted, password protected, or accessed through exploitation or trickery should be used. Things that exist in the public realm, no matter how difficult they are to find, are fair game. When I was in sales, I remember being hesitant to use any of the information I had obtained through examining a prospect's social presence in my conversations with the person. I didn't want my prospects to feel that I was violating their privacy or "watching" them in a creepy way. But when I started to slowly experiment with dropping relevant information I had gathered by these means, I was surprised at how receptive people were. I understand now, having been on the other end of this situation more than a few times, that people generally like it when others take the time to get to know them before approaching. It saves both parties a lot of unproductive time. People now expect you to do your homework first. Public biographical information is a great starting place, as well as the social content that people post. What are the themes that come up over and over again? Can you discern their goals and concerns from what they post? When do they seem to be taking a break from work and engaging in conversations? Write your observations down.

Second, read what they read. You wouldn't try to break into the film industry without reading *Variety*. Every tribe, tier, and niche has its core texts, and besides keeping people informed, they serve as conversation starters and idea disseminators, common points from which to start engaging and build relationships. Beyond that, knowing what someone reads can tell you a lot about who they are, and you may even find that you're already tuned into the same channels, so to speak. If you're trying to get access to a group of people, and not just an individual, pay attention to what members of the group share most often. Make a list of members of the group and then scan the content generated by the list for patterns and trends. For example, as part of my job, I spend a lot of my time trying to find new ways of reaching Fortune 500 marketing executives. I should make a Twitter list of all the people I can find in that category and then manually scan it or use a curation tool like Percolate's Daily Brew and News .me to find out what kind of articles they're sharing and which outlets they link to most often. (LinkedIn also has two useful free services, LinkedIn Today and Signals, where users can find the most popular links shared by industry, job type, group, and even company.) From there, I have the information I need to do a number of highly effective things to capture their attention and interest. I can place ads on the top 50 sites they link to, or I can secure byline articles and coverage on those sites. I can tell my salespeople to read those outlets regularly and reference them in sales conversations. I can thematically tailor the content I create and publish to reflect their interests, and I can even trim or extend the length of the content I'm putting out there to more closely mirror the average word count of the articles they typically tweet.

Third, before approaching someone, home in on those you both know and those you both follow. There are a few tools to help dig for shared social connections. For Twitter, followerwonk can show you the people that two or more accounts follow in common. I compared my account with Richard Branson's and found out that we both follow 58 Twitter users, many of whom I know well. If I ever need to contact him, I know just whom to approach. On LinkedIn, bringing up someone's profile can show you how you're connected to the person and by how many degrees. By viewing someone's Facebook profile, even if you're not yet friends, you can see how many mutual friends you have and who they are. The rest is networking basics. Ask for introductions, use references the person will recognize, and, when needed, call in favors. Despite its antiquity, "It's all about who you know" is still as true as it ever was, and we now have an array of tools at our disposal to discover shared connections. But maybe it requires some updating: "It's all about who follows you back."

Fourth, never doubt the power of shared interests and experiences—no matter how trivial. Anything has the potential to help you open a social media side door. Nowhere is this more evident than in Austin Gunter's story.

Austin is a friend of mine. He's constantly trying new things, exploring new corners of his mind, and expanding his tastes. Not too long ago, he was looking for a way into a job at Google (remember, Google gets 1 million applications per year on average).

Austin knew he needed a side door, so he decided to follow a few senior recruiters from Google on Twitter. Out of the blue one day, he got a DM from one of them about, of all things, yerba mate tea. Austin had included in his Twitter bio the fact that he enjoys drinking the South American tea, and a Google recruiter from Argentina had noticed. The friendly note kicked off a conversation about Austin's time in Chile—and within a few messages, his interest in working for Google. The recruiter happily passed Austin's résumé to another recruiter that day. Within a week, Austin had spoken to the second recruiter by phone. Seven weeks from that fateful DM about yerba mate tea, Austin had an offer from Google. Stories like Austin's are more common than you think. Find out what you have in common with the person or people you'll be approaching. There's always something you can use to break the ice and differentiate yourself.

Social intelligence gives you the edge you need to get on people's radar and stay engaged. It's also the wedge that separates you from the others vying for their attention. While your competitors are lining up at the front door to be ignored, you should be collecting social intelligence to open up the side door.

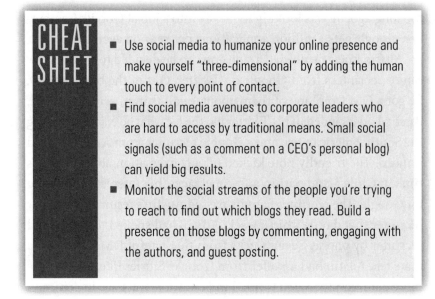

CHEAT SHEET

- Use social media to humanize your online presence and make yourself "three-dimensional" by adding the human touch to every point of contact.

- Find social media avenues to corporate leaders who are hard to access by traditional means. Small social signals (such as a comment on a CEO's personal blog) can yield big results.

- Monitor the social streams of the people you're trying to reach to find out which blogs they read. Build a presence on those blogs by commenting, engaging with the authors, and guest posting.

CHAPTER 3

I Hate "Networking"

The first blip on my Facebook timeline appeared in April 2005, back in the bad old days when only college students were allowed on the network. I was flirting with the person who would become my girlfriend a year later—and my wife six years after that. Looking through the years, I see interactions with and photos of a lot of people who were part of my life, many of whom are still part of my life. Moving from a small town in California to a big city in Texas, I used Facebook as my lifeline to my friends and family scattered across the globe. And as for the people I met along the way, Facebook gave us a logical starting place from which to build a relationship. What is Facebook's poke feature for, if not that? For all its silliness, it's one of the purest expressions of that desire to connect, however minimally, with other human beings—even when there's nothing yet to say. Likes, retweets, upvotes—these are all social signals that propel a relationship forward with little or no risk of verbal clumsiness, social anxiety, or misconstrued goals.

In one of the most touching blog posts I've ever read, a colleague of mine, Olivia Derr, described how social media helps people with severe social disorders, like her autistic son, with "a universe of comfortable social interaction" where the signals and protocols of communication are clear and finding people with similar interests is easy. I think even those of us who do not struggle with social interaction can celebrate these qualities of social media: For people who *are* natural connectors, it helps them connect even better.[1]

I'm passionate about these networks, and yet something about the term *networking* really turns me off. Whenever I hear it, I imagine a sterile room full of slick salespeople, dull careerists, stick-on name tags, and the robotic exchange of bone-white business cards. That kind of networking isn't my scene, and I'm particularly bad at it.

But networking happens. Against all odds, I've found myself with a large, influential circle of people whom I can call on when I need to. How did this happen to an introvert who struggles with face-to-face interaction, social anxiety, and an unrelenting clumsiness with small talk? Many in my situation find that drinks help them loosen up and connect; social media does the trick for me.

Relationships Are the Point

The reason networking can seem hollow is because it's so often calculated and superficial. Traditional networking frequently draws a hard line between personal and professional, and people can be reduced to nodes in a system—they are a means to your end; any real connection aside from that is beside the point, a perk at best. For most social media users, relationships *are* the point, and business and career gains are the occasional bonus.

Use social media enough, and you'll see people trying to use it like it was the chapter meeting of their boring networking club. They're pure opportunists, and they're the same people who sneered at the rise of social media, calling it a fad. Now they're trying to cash in, but they still don't get it. They're focusing solely on commercial opportunities, without putting in real work to build relationships that matter. I cataloged their species on my blog, bitter about the growing entitlement mentality I was seeing:

*And then you see those people with that look in their eye. It's not
determination, or a can-do freakin' attitude. It's the "how can
I use those in this room" look. They're the ones that approach
you because of who you work for or who you know, without any
thought as to who you are. All that matters to them is that you're
a potential asset. They don't ask you to grab coffee with them, they
expect you to. They talk more about themselves and their connections than they listen and learn. They tell you, flabbergasted, that
they applied for your job, but were rejected—and oh, by the way,
can you help them get another at your company?[2]*

And then there are the people who mean well but come off
as one-dimensional and too buttoned up. They don't let much of
themselves shine through, and it's hard for them to connect in any
meaningful way with others.

You don't have to be a master networker to succeed through
social media. You just have to want to meet cool people, you have to
want to learn, and you have to be willing to be yourself. As long as
you're doing that, opportunities will bubble up on occasion. If you're
there for the "right" reasons *and* actively looking for opportunities,
you'll find them everywhere.

Whatever Connects

When people are just getting into social media, they often ask me
what they're "supposed to be" doing. No matter their specific goals, I
begin by telling them, "Do whatever helps you connect with others."
Social media is so vast and so new and is in such a state of constant
change, formulas and step-by-step guides are only helpful as starting
points for the development of tailored strategies that reflect unique
goals, contexts, resources, and expertise. There is, however, one idea
that can be universalized as the basis of almost every successful
social strategy: relationships unlock opportunity.

Since we don't live in a meritocracy, relationships have always been important to achievement in nearly every realm. Success through social media is even more reliant on relationships for a few reasons. First and foremost, networks are built for the very purpose of linking people and things. Every burst of activity taking place on a network takes place in the context of a relationship: the relationship between originator and audience, between sharer and originator, between subject matter and audience, and so on. All connections are relationships, ranging from the fleeting and superficial to the lasting and intimate. Not every interaction you have will result in something fruitful, but social media allows for the growth of more relationships with less effort. Author Ted Rubin nails the concept:

> So can you maintain meaningful relationships with thousands of people at a time? No, but every touch is important, no matter how small. Think of it this way . . . individual touches are like relationship seeds. You have a much better likelihood of reaping a good harvest when you sow widely, but only if you prepare the ground with value and nurture with authenticity.[3]

Second, because social media is probably the first means of communication in which the vast majority of the communications are digitally archived, it acts as a kind of ledger that records the history of our relationships. And not just in the Library of Congress. Facebook's timeline is a great example because it allows users to go back to their very first moments on the network. Whom was I interacting with? What were we talking about? Oh God, was I *really* wearing that?

Third, social media is a landscape that can only be navigated through relationships. The fact that our access to people and information is now instant and global (or universal, taking into account Curiosity's Foursquare check-in on Mars and tweets from the

International Space Station) is a testament to the power of relationships. News of the Arab Spring reached most people by way of the ripple effect across overlapping social circles: I follow Tyler, but I don't follow Tariq. Tyler retweets Tariq, and now Tariq has entered my social circle. If I want to follow him and engage with him, I can make his place within that circle more permanent. Even news organizations on Twitter are now in the habit of retweeting first-person sources, rather than providing their own content—this is a convenient way of getting to stories quickly while placing the responsibility for veracity on the original sources. Those original sources enter your stream, and thus your social circle, only because someone you choose to follow has chosen to relay them to you as part of her audience. Ever see a bubble split into two bubbles? It's like that in reverse.

Spending time with speakers on the social media conference circuit, one often sees a big difference between their social media and in-person interactions. Though this is an effect that is present in our society in general today, it's especially apparent in this circle. The most digitally outgoing people can seem reserved at mixers; folks who are "all business" online will often show an edgier side at group dinners. This isn't disingenuous; it's a reflection of a new reality in which social media helps us to grow into the people we want to be. People who get tongue-tied or sheepish but *want* to change themselves for the better can start with their social media selves, where it's much easier to begin. It makes you wonder what skills are transferring from the digital realm to other areas of life. Does tweeting to thousands of followers every day make a person more comfortable speaking to a crowd of a few hundred strangers? Do a person's interactions in social media make that person's everyday encounters a little easier? In my life the answer has been yes, and I know I'm not alone.

Social media, then, is aspirational. It can help you become a better version of yourself. The skills you cultivate are transferable.

A Better Starting Point

Social media is a springboard from which to launch relationships.
It used to be that when we met people professionally, we might slip
their business card into the Rolodex, where it would gather dust
until we needed something from them. Now, professionally and in
other contexts, the first step is to friend or to follow, accompanied
perhaps with an e-mailed "great to meet you" note.

Thus the frequency of interaction and exposure increases.
Through automatically updating feeds, we see our network's activity stream hum along, with or without us. We can tune in and just
experience it, catching the odd update of someone we haven't seen
in person for years. Or we can jump in and engage with someone we
just met; liking a post or retweeting the person's content is a social
act accompanied by far less baggage than a phone call or e-mail.
Such effortless social actions are noncommittal and nonintrusive,
so they happen more frequently.

The exploratory phase is always the most awkward part of any
new relationship. It's that period when you're looking for common
ground, engaging primarily in casual question-and-answer to find
that piece of information that can form a touchstone between both
parties. Whether it's a shared favorite sports team, beloved foreign
locale, or preferred airline, you're both looking for something that
can be discussed with ease and without the constant mental refrain
of "What am I going to say next?" Until you get there, the road is
bumpy. But it can be exciting, too. When you find that touchstone,
all the self-aware, deliberate aspects of conversation that make it
stilted and uncomfortable melt into the background, and a genuine
channel is opened. The problem for people like me is that we don't
naturally possess the endurance and patience to get there; you'll
catch us fleeing the scene at the first awkward pause, verbal fum-
ble, or perceived negative nonverbal cue. Social media makes the
exploratory phase easier, with far fewer awkward moments. As you

and I are first connecting, I learn that you are also a fan of the novelist Daniel Woodrell, and I didn't even ask you about your favorite authors. That information is in your profile, or you like Woodrell's page, and I catch it by chance in my Facebook news feed. This continual accrual of touchstones is both active (seeking) and passive (observing); it's a fundamental part of the social media experience. Knowing what I know now, I have something else to talk to you about without having first to extract it from you through the tedious hit-and-miss exercise that used to be such a daunting part of socializing to so many. Armed with the information I need to talk to you about stuff you actually care about, I can swiftly take our engagement to the next level.

The Ledger

All social platforms allow for at least some relationship time traveling. The record of the relationship (though not always to its inception) is there for examination and reference. Most people don't actively seek out the ledger, but it manifests everywhere. Send someone a message on Facebook, and you'll see the other messages you've sent to them. Twitter makes sure you know if someone is following you or not. Social media makes it easier than ever to answer the question, "What have you done for me lately?" If you're requesting something from someone, do you follow him on Twitter? Have you linked to his content? Have you shared it? Do you share contacts? These are all potential considerations one might make when evaluating your request.

When I sold marketing services to real estate agents, I learned the importance of this ledger. One of the first things I would do when approaching prospects was to map out their social presence. I would find whichever platform they seemed to be most comfortable on, and then I'd engage there before calling. It wasn't about what I was selling, either. Sometimes it was as simple as retweeting a post of theirs that I agreed with. Other times, I would comment on a blog post of theirs. I found that if I sent these positive social signals in their direction before I called, I could refer to the interactions at the outset of the call and get a warm reception:

> *Hi, Charlene. This is Ian Greenleigh—I commented on that post you wrote last week about working with out-of-state buyers. I think you really hit the nail on the head there, and I wanted to call and introduce myself.*

Whether people remembered the initial interaction or not, it was on the record for me to reference and for them to verify.

This method was even more effective when *they* had commented on *my* blog, because it told me that they were interested in my point of view, and so I would call to carry the conversation beyond the blog post:

> *Hi there, Marcos. My name's Ian Greenleigh; you commented on my blog post about mobile strategies for brokers, and I wanted to thank you for that comment and introduce myself.*

Thousands of calls began like this, and the strategy worked phenomenally well. After the initial greeting, I'd invite these people to an upcoming webinar or ask if I could send them some information about what I did, but I never jumped into hard-sell mode in that first conversation, because I wanted to continue to add to that relationship ledger. I'd stay on their radar through low-effort social interactions, sharing their content, adding them on other networks, and continuing to comment on their blog. And every time I called, they knew who I was. I started to get inbound calls from real estate agents who were referred by people who weren't even my customers yet—just social contacts of mine who knew my work. Relationships are investments that will pay dividends as long as one sustains them.

Circles of Empathy

According to author and psychologist Steven Pinker:

> *Evolution bequeathed us with a sense of empathy. Unfortunately,*
> *by default we apply it equally to a narrow circle of friends and*
> *family. But over the course of history you can see the circle of*
> *empathy expanding to embrace not just the family but the village*
> *and the clan, then the tribe, then the nation, then it's extended*
> *to other races, to both sexes, to children, and eventually to other*
> *sentient beings, other species.*[4]

This helps explain the role of the Internet and social media in the color revolutions and the Arab Spring, posits Pinker. Indeed, two of the catalysts for increasing empathy are "technologies that increase cosmopolitanism" and "reading a person's words." Porter Gale observes that since social media provides both these catalysts, our "circle of empathy" is expanding. In other words, we are empathizing with more people than ever before due largely to social media. Even the way we imagine some of the people in our lives is changing:

> *Think about in the past when you would think about relationships*
> *and connections, your image of a person might have been the last*
> *time you saw them at a dinner party. Now, because of technology*
> *and also because of reading about history, and literature, and all*
> *sorts of things, our last impression of somebody might be a tweet,*
> *might be a post.*[5]

Empathy is critical to the formation of meaningful relationships. We have the capacity to care about people we have never met before, and that capacity is growing. To an outsider, not familiar with the ins and outs of social media, this seems strange or even absurd. But when people open up online, it's harder and harder not to empathize—not to feel *something*. You can't help but experience a small part of what they're experiencing as they live their lives and share some of it, or all of it, with the world.

The Empathy Graph

If the social graph plots the people you know and if the interest graph maps your interests, then the empathy graph is the map of your emotional connections to others. "As it turns out, sometimes strangers are more supportive than friends," writes M. Sinclair Stevens. "Our social graph relationships are mostly accidents of proximity. Do we want to be stuck with people just because our paths crossed once upon a time?" Like the social and interest graphs, you already have one, and it expands and contracts in real time.

The good news for people looking for access and influence is that empathy is one of the best door openers out there. Gatekeepers and those on the other side of the door have it, and they use it to guide some of their decisions. Remembering when they had themselves suffered through a spate of rejections, they may lend a young job seeker a hand. Or seeing how passionate you are about a topic they care about, too, they may open up the lines of communication. If you appear on their empathy graph, chances are, you're getting through the door.

Rewarding the Real You

Besides professionally oriented networks like LinkedIn, social media use is an activity that takes place during free time for average users, but it's consuming a lot of their day: in 2012, 27 percent of U.S., U.K., and Australian online PC activity, and 15 percent of U.S. mobile browsing, took place on social networks, according to Experian.[6] And although this means it's bleeding into our workday—6 in 10 employees use social media while at work—social media's informal roots will always shape its use.[7] It is still more of a friendly dinner party than a stuffy board meeting, despite the laudable adoption of social media by businesses around the world.

My twitter handle, @be3d, is shorthand for "be three-dimensional." It's the principle that has helped me and millions of others truly get somewhere with social media. It doesn't matter whether your goals are purely business oriented or not; in social media, your audience determines your path to success. That audience is still made up of people being themselves online and expecting the same from you. No one wants to form a relationship with people who only show them one perfectly positioned, expertly scrubbed side of their lives. Incomplete or manufactured personas are difficult to empathize with, but it's easy to connect with real people.

Social media affords us far more opportunity to connect than the physical world does. Even in a large American city, it can be difficult to find and engage with people who share particular interests. If Rule 34 of the Internet is, "If it exists, there's porn of it," Rule 35 might be, "If you're interested in it, you'll find an online social community for it." Maybe it's a blog with a vibrant commenter and author community. Or it's a Facebook page dedicated to something you love. Or it might be something more ephemeral, like a Twitter hashtag. Whatever it is, there's a social community for it—somewhere for you to connect with people who share your affinities. That means that being three-dimensional on social networks can yield better results than it does in the physical world: the probability of connecting with likeminded others is higher. And even if you and someone else don't share interests or other touchstones, being yourself gives off an inviting, likable quality that people find refreshing and attractive.

Who Cares?

Networks like Twitter can seem daunting at first. What can I, as 1 user out of 500 million, say that hasn't been said? Why would anyone care what I think about anything? But your audience isn't 500 million. It's only the people you care to connect with; however small or large you make this group is up to you. Returning home from college to my small town in California, where everyone knows everyone else, people would ask me how I could possibly enjoy being 1 out of more than 40,000 students. I'd tell them I didn't look at it like that. I was 1 of a few thousand government majors, 1 of 5 or 6 opinion columnists for *The Daily Texan*, 1 of 20 students in my beginner's tennis class—my life was (and is) made up of concentric social circles of various sizes. I never thought of myself as struggling to find an identity in 40,000; I was simply enjoying the fact that there were thousands of people who shared at least one of my passions, all within a radius of a few miles. I didn't need to venture far before I would see a flyer for something that captured my interest, an opportunity to connect with others like me. And I didn't need to change who I was to fit in to a predetermined "scene." That's the beauty of social media: community is dynamic, accessible, and instant. There are no entrance fees or litmus tests. There are no rulers. Just people drawn together by shared interests, proximity, and friendship—and often a strange, beautiful blend of all three.

Touchstones

When I was selling custom-designed blogs, I searched for tweets that indicated a need for blog designers. I remember meeting someone this way that epitomized just how strong a niche the connective tissue of social media can create. It was a young college student with a Tumblr blog, and he was looking for an upgrade. His blog was devoted to clean, Mormon-themed humor for the college set; kind of a sanitized play on the "shit my dad says" meme. I thought, "There's no way this guy has any budget for this; the traffic stats are low, and the site isn't ad supported." I was wrong. This "LDS humor" blog had already raised enough for a decent overhaul from its cadre of devoted fans. On a national level, or probably even a Utah-wide level, this blog didn't even register a blip. But it struck the right chord with enough people who were living through a shared experience, and they were willing to invest in its future.

Social media runs on touchstones. At no time is this more evident than when traveling abroad, searching for local tips on cuisine and worthwhile attractions. Even in tiny countries like Belize and St. Maarten, expatriates connect through vibrant social conversations. They congregate on blogs, discussing issues ranging from the trivial to the serious, exchange insider tips, and let outsiders like me scoop up the local wisdom for my own purposes. They connect for many reasons, but chief among them is the universal, human need to relate to others and to find a common starting place from which to do so. In this case, it's a shared expatriate history and a desire to belong; in others, it's a favorite television show, football team, or author. For all of our remarkable complexity as a species, one common factor is all it takes for a community to emerge.

Social media makes finding connection points with people much easier. You may have a point of view of something they've written about, an experience with something they've tweeted, or an answer to a question they've posed on LinkedIn. If you don't, it might be worth reevaluating whether the people you're trying to approach are really all that influential and whether you have anything to offer that will make the prospect of engaging with you worthwhile for them. But ordinarily there's no need to grasp at possible connection points when the interest graph is right in front of you. When I asked James Buckhouse, who works on Twitter's corporate design team, if he had any advice for using Twitter to open social media side doors, his reply was simple: "Instead I'd recommend sticking to the basics: follow people you find interesting; tweet messages that others would want to repeat; explore hashtags to find new voices on topics you love." My relationships with influencers tend to start by reading their blog posts and chiming in when I have something to add, and often when I find a point on which we disagree. Nothing grabs attention in the sometimes saccharine-sweet world of social media like dissent. If it is presented in a way that's thoughtful and constructive, dissent can be wonderfully effective. For example, here's an early interaction I had with author and analyst Brian Solis (in the post, he's lamenting the fact that businesses are launching social profiles without clear strategies behind them):

> Me: *"Every brand believes that simply creating these presences is all that's required to 'win.'" A bit of an overstatement, no? I agree that this is generally true, but examples of the "good" brand abound. Social media is word of mouth. All the data you cite above is further evidence of this.*
>
> Brian: *Duly noted . . . changed "every" to "many"—and that's just based on the companies that I've worked with and those I've interviewed over the years. Thanks Ian.*[8]

My critique led Brian to rethink something he had written, alter it, and thank me publicly. The next time I made a comment, I'm sure he paid a little more attention to it—I had proved that I had an interesting perspective worth considering. My relationship with Brian evolved from those simple comments; it jumped channels to e-mail, to in-person chats at conferences, and to several guest posts on his wildly popular blog. It continues to grow, and I'm proud that he was one of the first people to give me notes on the proposal I put together for the book you're reading now.

Ask Yourself This

At times, social media can act as a bit of a "relationship distortion field." The general positivity and sunny ethos of most social circles can make relationships seem more substantive than they really are, when the rubber hits the road. There's also a tendency for people to mistake positive social signals for permission to ask too much of people and too soon. As Clay Shirky put it to me:

> It's easier to ask a question than to answer one. Something is coming, because it cannot be the case that you can simultaneously hugely increase participatory opportunity without automatically creating a world in which many more people turn down many more people. The current model of politeness in our society doesn't deal with that very well.

To avoid putting someone in this awkward position, before you're about to ask for something, ask yourself this: Would I feel comfortable picking up the phone and doing this? And if so, how would I expect people to respond? Keep in mind that the standards you should use to evaluate whether and when to approach someone should vary depending on the networks through which you're connected. Networks like Facebook and LinkedIn are primarily oriented around the social graph, so actually knowing someone will make your request more viable. Networks like Twitter and many blog communities are based on the interest graph, so having a shared passion, interest, need, or goal will count more on those networks than on networks based on social connections.

Social Discovery

I was in London for business, staying in a neighborhood not known for its nightlife. I had been too busy with work to plan any leisure or social activities in advance of my stay, so I hopped online to look for something to do. The jet lag was clouding my memory—did I know anyone living in London? I pulled up LinkedIn, filtered my contacts by location, and saw that an old high school friend had just moved to London. Figuring he'd be as interested to explore the city as I was, I messaged him and got a reply a few minutes later. We met up the following evening and had a blast and then did it again the next night. It's pretty astonishing to consider the fact that a free service, LinkedIn, led to this reconnection—one that made my trip much more fun.

Social discovery happens when you encounter (or rediscover) something because of your connections to other people, interests, or circumstances. Spotify shows you what music your friends are listening to. Foursquare tells you about the current check-in hotspots in your city. Chill serves up videos your friends have liked. These are all great applications of social discovery technology, but its real promise is as the starting point for new and stronger relationships. Whom should you meet? What do you have in common with the people in the room?

Imagine you're at a giant conference, and you have on your smartphone the social discovery app of the near future. You don't know anyone there, but you'd like to meet people. Where to begin? You pull up your app, and it tells you that 50 other Texas Longhorn alumni are at the conference, gives you links to their social profiles, and provides a way to message them all at once—something like, "UT Alumni Meetup at [name of nearby bar], 6pm." The app also monitors for shared connections to people who have checked into the convention center on location apps or have RSVP'd to the event on LinkedIn. Turns out there's one person in particular who knows a lot of the same people you know, and she works for a company you've been trying to earn business with for a while now. You ping her to see if she has time to meet up tomorrow, and then you check to see if the social content you and she post, respectively, reveals any commonalities. A few minutes later, you receive an alert on your phone that someone you didn't expect to see at the conference, a Twitter connection who always shares interesting content, has arrived. This one app has given you several social options in the space of an hour.

All these social discovery features exist, but not on the same app—yet. The most basic social discovery function can answer questions like, "Whom should I follow?" and "Which of my contacts are on this network?" Twitter suggests people and hashtags to follow based on the people I follow. Facebook lets me search for friends with their names or e-mail addresses, and many networks offer ways to automate this process by searching through my contacts for users with accounts. LinkedIn tells me if I have any shared connections with someone who is not yet a direct connection.

Strong relationships are built on multiple connection points. Social discovery's job, then, is to expose the connection points that already exist, not to forge them. As Matthew Grant writes:

> *Social media doesn't create the commonalities. It doesn't spin the yarn or tell the tale. But by shining the light, by providing the campfire around which the song can be sung, it facilitates communion and, if we're lucky, helps us build the communities of interest and mutual benefit that are at the heart of true commerce.*[9]

An End to Serendipity?

I used to wonder if our collective obsession with data might eliminate the joy of serendipity from life. If we have more and more data about the world around us and about those with whom we pass through it, more of our behavior can be calculated to lead to desirable outcomes. But does this leave much room for those unexpected moments that make life special or for the connections with others that emerge organically? Who and what are we tuning out when we use apps to maximize the "return" on time spent building relationships? If social discovery is used primarily as a filter, there will always be the risk that people and things we would like to encounter will never reach us. But if it is used as a lens that helps us highlight and unearth things we might ordinarily miss, then it becomes a *means* to serendipity—and that's something to celebrate, not fear.

One of my favorite examples of the intersection of social discovery and serendipity comes from Porter Gale:

Last year, a week prior to a speech I was to give in Budapest, I posted on my Facebook page, "Do any of you have connections in or recommendations for Budapest?" Instantly, an e-mail arrived: "I know the U.S. ambassador to Hungary. She's in Budapest. I'll see if she'll have lunch with you." Within 48 hours, I had a lunch secured with Ambassador Eleni Tsakopoulos Kounalakis.[10]

A practice I always try to stick to is thanking the person who connects me to something or someone new—even if this social discovery was passive (i.e., you didn't request a connection but found it some other way, such as through the Spotify feed of what your friends are listening to). These simple gestures are easy, and they help strengthen existing relationships. Doing this publicly is also a great way to get on the radar of a new person in your network, by offering social proof of a mutual relationship.

Best Of/Worst Of

You don't have to venture far to find the worst of human nature refracted across social media. I admit that my outrage has been depleted due to repeat exposure to all manner of nastiness and ignorance. Anonymity, distance, projection—they each contribute poison to the well when used to harm others.

But the well is larger than we can imagine with our limited perspectives and brainpower. The well is where people gather, collaborate, empathize, discuss, dream, and relate. The well reflects the entire spectrum of humanity, but also the spectrum of human relationships. It is social in the same way humans have always been social. We're able to socialize with people on every level, from superficial to intimate. We never have the full story, do we? We don't know what happens after witnessing a back-and-forth exchange on Twitter; perhaps nothing, perhaps something more we'll never see. It's hard to build relationships 140 characters at a time, but I think we're getting better at it.

CHEAT SHEET

- Opportunity follows relationship, not the other way around. Many people and businesses reverse this order and fail.
- Seek touchstones upon which to build relationships initially—shared interests, experiences, contacts, etc. The vastness and public nature of social networks make it easier than ever before to connect with people on the basis of shared affinity.
- Circles of empathy are expanding—social media can make us care about people we've never met. Even gatekeepers use empathy as the basis for some of their decisions.
- Sometimes, the best way to get people's attention is to respectfully disagree with them in public—like on their blog.

CHAPTER 4

Walking Through the Social Media Side Door

I t began with a tweet:

I'd like to see more books w/ official hashtags so readers can discuss while reading. Not just SM [social media] books. [1]

A fleeting idea . . . or so I thought. Several people retweeted it within the hour, so I decided to blog about the idea. Weeks passed with little activity on the post. Then, out of the blue, a Twitter friend of mine e-mailed the iconic author Seth Godin about the idea and introduced us. The next day, Seth blogged about it, linked to my post, and assigned official hashtags to the three most recent books from his imprint.[2] Since then, we've kept in touch, I interviewed him in a blog post, and he provided advanced praise for this book. If that didn't feel surreal enough, a coworker of mine visited my desk and plunked down a copy of Seth's book *We Are All Weird*. Printed on the back was the book's official hashtag. I'll never forget that moment—and that it all started with a tweet.

Access is either active or passive. Active access is the deliberate and direct pursuit of entry. Reaching out to someone directly through LinkedIn to request a lunch meeting is active access. Tweeting at an editor and asking her to read your book proposal is active access (no, I don't make that a habit). Active access is sometimes risky. Your cards are on the table. You're knocking on the door and asking to be let in. It's easy to find your approach a bit jarring or abrasive. Who is this person again? What does he want? And why is he tweeting at me? On the other hand, it's hard to ignore someone being so direct.

Passive access is earned over time, and sometimes it's unexpected. Maybe one of your blog readers is organizing a conference you didn't even know about, and he or she thinks you'd be a great speaker. The event's attendees are exactly the kind of people you're trying to get in front of. Passive access is like being invited in, as opposed to requesting an invite. It's built through steady engagement with decision makers and the people they trust, and it is focused on making true contributions before making any self-interested requests.

But you don't have to choose between active and passive access. They aren't mutually exclusive; they're actually quite complimentary. My access to Seth Godin, for example, started out as passive and moved steadily to active. The trick is to build the pathway. Start with a passive approach, earning mindshare and influence, until you feel confident that the people you're reaching out to directly will know who you are and will want to help you out. If you've been giving more than you've been taking at that point—sharing or creating great content, helping them spread their ideas, engaging with them on a regular basis—your direct approach will seem like a natural next step, and you'll get more of their attention and consideration.

Before Klout Was Cool

Back in 2009, I wasn't yet a marketer. But I was curious about marketing, about social media, and I blogged because I had ideas worth sharing. That year, I wrote a post called "What Klout Can't Calculate: Dimensions of Influence." The post centered on the argument that Klout, founded just a year earlier, did not "track the offline influence of online personalities." In other words, its service wasn't measuring holistically. A Fortune 50 CEO with no social footprint is, all things considered, more influential than a blogger with a high Klout score; yet within Klout, that CEO would score low. The very first comment on that post—on a blog with almost no influence, mind you—was from Klout's CEO, Joe Fernandez. It wasn't defensive or rude; it actually made a lot of sense:

> *Hi, my name is Joe Fernandez and I am the CEO and co-founder at Klout. Thank you for checking out what we are working on! You're absolutely right, we (and other online tools) are only getting part of the story when it comes to identifying influencers. Warren Buffett, for example, is way more influential than any person we might rank as highly influential about the stock market or investing. We see our data as a way to augment or balance the "human touch" that will always be needed to identify influencers. Great article and thanks again for checking out what we are working on!*

I had no idea how notable Klout, or Joe, would become, and it *still* felt so cool for the cofounder of a hot start-up to care what I thought, especially since he seemed to consider my critique valid. But the story doesn't end there. I kept in touch with Joe, casually. We'd exchange tweets here and there, but that was the extent of it, until I had an idea for a research project at Bazaarvoice that would benefit from some of Klout's data. Since he had commented on my blog several years ago, I had his e-mail address. I arranged a meeting with Joe, visited Klout's office in San Francisco, and got the collaboration rolling. Later, I was working on a video interview series that profiled start-up founders and marketing thought leaders. One of the topics we wanted to explore was the changing nature of influence, and Joe was a natural fit. Again, I reached out to Joe and arranged a visit, this time with our in-house video producer and a carful of video and lighting gear. These two massive opportunities, on both personal and professional levels, wouldn't have happened without the social media side door I created without even realizing it at the time.

Sometimes the most rewarding access is indirect, delayed, or unexpected. While it may seem a bit karmic, it's really just a balance sheet. If you continually deliver value to the audience you're cultivating, every so often a social media side door will open. You'll think about all the times you doubted whether you were creating anything worthwhile—anything worthy of the world's attention. And then you'll smile and get back to work.

The Social Proof Imperative

I was once told a bit of corporate lore that stuck with me, even though I haven't been able to verify it (please tweet me if you can substantiate this!). A woman who did some consulting work for GE told me that when she exchanged cards with people around the company, she noticed the cards ranged in stock from standard to extremely thick. When she asked another consultant who had worked with GE for several years why this was, she learned that it was a subtle way to signal seniority within the GE corporate hierarchy. The thicker the card, the more important the person. At an organization the size of GE, with such a vast array of divisions and job titles, the stock of one's business card can be a shortcut meant to convey necessary information quickly and without much thought.

Can you imagine looking for a new car by literally considering every brand and model on the market, then whittling your options down from there? It would be a long, boring, grueling process. In reality, we prefilter some options out by eliminating cars that don't meet our specific needs, such as SUVs with low gas mileage or cars that don't match our aesthetic tastes.

Another mental shortcut is equally helpful, but we're less conscious of it. We also prefilter options by thinking about what *other people* are buying and then by favoring those cars over others. Beginning last year, for example, my friends and family started buying Hyundai cars, a brand I had always considered "cheap," in a pejorative sense. But my sentiment toward the brand is now vastly improved, and it would be near the top of my list for my next car. Why?

These mental shortcuts are called *heuristics*. They help us be more efficient with brainpower and are critical to our survival; we simply can't fully analyze every possible course of action in each situation we encounter—there aren't enough hours in the day. Instead, we use heuristics such as social proof, which we use to decide what to do (or what to think) based on what we see others doing. Advertisers and marketers have long known that people don't trust them, so they leverage our natural use of the social proof heuristic by offering testimonials and endorsements from third parties. They also try to "trick" our social proof triggers by featuring actors in ads that are ostensibly "like us"—young mothers in diaper commercials, for instance.

Traditional endorsements are specific and direct; I ask for a quote from my best customers, or I pay a celebrity to pretend he likes what I sell. Or when I'm looking for a job, I ask my former colleagues for references (this has been updated with the advent of LinkedIn recommendations, but it's the same practice).

Endorsements can be tacit and subtle, too. This is the kind of social proof that typically exists in the social web, and it's critical to opening up side doors. After all, an endorsement doesn't have to be explicit. Just ask any reporter or blogger about the bad PR pitches they get. Here's one:

> SPOTTED: *Sexy actress Olivia Munn shopping for Tropicana Trop50 Orange Juice drink in NYC.*[3]

Did Olivia Munn endorse this diet OJ? No. But the mere fact that someone snapped a photo of her buying it was good enough for PR flacks to use it, because it may work. People don't need to consciously put two and two together to have a more positive sentiment toward the Trop50 brand—our unconscious often takes over. It's a particularly egregious example of a common phenomenon that rules the social web. Some of the social proof signals that people rely on for mental shortcuts—whether they admit it or not—include:

- Number of social connections (Twitter followers, Facebook friends, etc.)
- Mentions and links in social content (tweets, blog posts, comments, etc.)
- Evidence of high traffic to blog or website
- List and RSS subscribers
- Klout score

All these signals convey information. Someone having a high number of Twitter followers or blog subscribers means, on the face of it, a lot of people care to listen to her. Social proof is the mechanism that kicks in once we see this, the feeling that *we* should give her our attention as well. If we were to evaluate whether or not to pay attention to people by sifting through every social signal they emit, our social circle would necessarily be tiny.

Although they do make impressions on people, raw numbers aren't the best indicators of importance. Subscribers, links, friends, and followers can all be gamed. So can the algorithms that suck in disparate information and spit out Klout scores. The strongest signal when it comes to social proof is influence by association. This happens when someone who is already an influencer publicly engages with you. Maybe this person retweets something you posted, mentions you on his blog, or "loves" your Instagram photo. In doing so, he passes on influence to you. The people in his audience are now aware of you and of the fact that someone who influences them is taking the time to engage with you. If you're on the influencer's radar, so the mental math goes, you should be on the audience's radar, too.

Using social proof to your advantage isn't as simple as amplifying this social proof, but doing this can help a bit. There's a way to do it tastefully, in moderation. You could set up a "press room" on your website with digital clippings of the coverage you've received; links to the original content pass on SEO value to the source. Or you could promote the fact that someone influential included you on a list by retweeting the post with a note of thanks, which might send some traffic the person's way. But all you're really doing here in terms of social proof is signaling to followers that they should think even more highly of you. This is really just a "humble brag," defined by *Urban Dictionary* as, "When you, usually consciously, try to get away with bragging about yourself by couching it in a phony show of humility."[4] The Twitter account of the same name finds and retweets humble brags in the wild, like this one:

> *Very humbled to be selected for the TIME 100 this year! Had a nice evening at their gala, but their standards . . . fb.me/1zh1QVZsW*[5]

But humble bragging won't cut it. To earn substantial social proof, you need to work on building your network, promoting the work of others, starting conversations, sharing and creating interesting content, and figuring out what you, uniquely, can bring to the table through social media. The more value you provide to your audience, the larger and faster your arsenal of social proof will grow. That's when the mentions, links, shares, and quotes start to pile up, and the social proof you've accumulated can blast the locks off the social media side doors in your life.

Befriending the Doorman

I was trying everything under the sun to start a dialogue with a certain social influencer who will remain unnamed. This person was a bit of a kingmaker: I had heard that anyone he tweeted about would gain hundreds of followers overnight. Turns out this wasn't really true, but I believed it at the time. At that point in my career, I had joined the growing chorus of strategists who claimed follower counts were bogus indicators of importance or influence, something that I truly believed. And yet, bigger still seemed better. What's more, this person had the ear of senior marketing decision makers in the Fortune 500, my company's market, who turned to this person for vendor selection advice. Motivated by both the personal and the professional, I devoted significant time and energy to getting on this person's radar. I tried to talk to the person at industry events like South by Southwest and was given short shrift. But despite my intelligent, pithy, timely responses to this person's tweets (at least that's how I saw them), and other efforts, like linking to and quoting this person on our blog, I received absolutely no signals that I was getting through. At least I could take solace in the fact that I wasn't the only one trying and failing at this task—a search of the person's Twitter handle showed an absurdly selective ratio of mentions to responses—my tweets, however brilliant they may have been, were lost in the cacophony of thousands of chirps for attention.

I was about to give up when, out of the blue, another influencer mentioned me in a tweet. It was someone whom I had never met, and had interacted with on only a few occasions. This person was paying more attention to the content I was creating and sharing than I would have ever guessed, and the tweet was about some of the social media experts he respected. There was my handle, alongside those of 11 others, all of them highly renowned for their thoughts and work in the space. It seemed almost laughable to put me in such company, but I soon learned that all that really mattered was that *this person* felt I should be among them.

That single tweet turned everything around. Suddenly, I started getting responses from the person I was trying to reach, tweets that indicated that this individual valued what I had to say. It wasn't my content or approach that changed—it was this person's perception of me, after seeing that I was respected by someone this person respected. Today, I'm good friends with both of these people. Whereas before I detected elitism in the influencer's cold shoulder, I now understand that I was one of hundreds, maybe thousands, of people simultaneously vying for attention. This person relied on social proof signals, out of necessity, to decide whom to listen to.

Social proof works upstream, too. If you can't get in front of someone directly, befriend the people who can help you get access. This is the digital version of "knowing a guy that knows a guy." In my life, the most tangible examples of this have been "plus-one" invites to exclusive events. It wasn't the organizers who invited me, but invited guests who knew me through social media (often people I had never met) and had a plus one to burn. My presence at these events then became further social proof that I "belonged" in that circle, that I was someone worth meeting. And so I have often been able to engage with people who are hard to reach without an "in," which means that they are now my first-degree connections—and now I am the "doorman" for others hoping for an introduction. In a way, that makes me a gatekeeper.

It's the same principle behind the everyday practice of introducing someone to someone else you know. If friend A wanted to meet friend B, A could approach B directly, but it may be slightly awkward or unexpected. But if I introduce friend A to friend B by sending a signal to B such as, "This is my friend A; she's doing some really interesting work I think you'll want to hear about," friend A will be received in a much warmer fashion.

Find your doorman. He or she may be someone you already know or perhaps someone you have yet to meet. I won't moralize by saying that you shouldn't use people to get access—you already know that, and most people can sniff out this behavior. But there's nothing wrong with looking for new ways to get more out of a relationship, as long as you're conscious of what you're bringing to the table to make it more equitable.

The Myth of Reciprocity

Social media platforms are frequently lumped together as if they all operate in the same way. But the culture of each is in reality very distinct, especially when it comes to the ideas of reciprocity.

Rules of etiquette are shaped by the ways people use things. Facebook operates primarily on the social graph: People friend people they know personally. Both parties must agree to connect. That's why ignoring or rejecting friend requests can be a nail-biting decision—they are from people you actually know, and doing so may personally offend them.

LinkedIn operates on the social graph: people generally connect because they have worked together in some capacity, have had another type of business relationship, or are connected through a mutual contact. (Of course, more and more are using it as a sales tool to communicate with prospects they *don't* know, but uninvited communications from strangers are not the norm.) Since the common goal of LinkedIn users is to network for business, ignoring or rejecting friend requests can be counterproductive.

On both LinkedIn and Facebook, it's best not to place people in awkward situations by trying to befriend those you don't actually know.

Twitter is an entirely different beast. First, it is based on the interest graph, which means people primarily use it to find out more about their interests. Following people on Twitter is usually predicated on whether or not their content interests you, not whether or not you know them personally. The etiquette of Twitter doesn't involve a lot of reciprocity—if you follow me, I'm not expected to follow you; and if you tweet a link to my blog, I shouldn't feel obligated to do the same for you.

And yet, on Twitter, those with high followed-to-following ratios can be labeled elitists or snobs. But the reality is that we only have so many hours in the day to absorb updates, so being selective is perfectly natural and shouldn't be considered snobbish. If someone won't follow you back, don't ever take it personally.

Platforms aside for a moment, the expectation of reciprocity itself is a bit of a sham. There used to be an SEO technique that was all about exchanging links (it still goes on today, but it's far less effective). I would approach you and ask if you would link from your site to mine in exchange for linking from my site to yours. Google and other search engines would then "see" that you are linking to me, and in a sense vouching for my content, and I would appear higher in the results rankings. They would also see my link to your site and bump you up, too. The problem with this scheme was twofold. First, if my site was seen as more important by a search engine, I would be giving you far more value than you would be giving me. Second, search engines began to penalize sites that had too many outbound links for essentially gaming the system. It was never as simple as "a link for a link."

The same applies to social media. One party is almost always in a more powerful position. It's not fair to expect someone to mention or follow you, for example, simply because you mentioned or followed that person. It's often a bigger spend of influence on the person's end as well. If I am following 500 people and am followed by 1,000, and Katy Perry is following 120 people and is followed by 36,000,000, everyone she follows will receive a huge amount of social proof, while I give Perry hardly any social proof by following her.

Imagine if people always felt obligated to return the favor in social media. Would people actually be interesting if they had to share other people's content out of some sense of reciprocity? Would it be as special when you get followed, friended, or mentioned by someone that you admire?

The best way to get on an influencer's radar is still to positively differentiate yourself by giving them something that others don't.

Becoming Indispensable

in·dis·pen·sa·ble/ˌindiˈspensəbəl/
Adjective:
Absolutely necessary or essential.

Whom and what do you consider indispensable? Friends you turn to for advice when you're not sure which path to take? The cup of coffee that delivers that rush of caffeine to start your day? Your iPhone?

Yes, you could technically survive without these people or things. But your life may be tougher, less fun, and even less fulfilling. That's the thing about being indispensable: it's always relative.

Social media can help make you or your company indispensable as a source of . . .

- Knowledge
- Connections
- Expertise
- Insight
- Guidance
- Perspective
- Humor
- Motivation
- Energy

And a whole lot more.

Brian Stelter became indispensable. The *New York Times* star reporter didn't ask for anyone's permission to become a journalist, and he didn't wait for a degree. He originally launched *CableNewser* in 2004, during his first year at Towson University, "to track cable news coverage of the [Iraq] invasion."[6] The blog was soon renamed *TVNewser,* and it grew in both scope and popularity while expanding its coverage to the cable news industry in general. In 2006, the

New York Times profiled *TVNewser* and its creator in a piece that spoke of Stelter as a kind of symbol of the democratizations of influence and access:

> *Perhaps this is what the techno-geeks had in mind when they invented the Internet—a device to squash not only time and space, but also social class and professional hierarchies, putting an unprepossessing Maryland college student with several term papers due in a position to command the attention and grudging respect of some of society's most famous and powerful personalities.*[7]

Less than a year later, and just three months after graduating from Towson, the *Times* hired Stelter as a media reporter. *TVNewser* became indispensable, he told me, because "it served as an industry bulletin board, something every industry wants and needs."

I asked Stelter if he thought it was ironic that the very people who were reading his blog—"network presidents, media executives, producers and publicists," as the *New York Times* described them in an internal memo upon his arrival—were themselves media gatekeepers?

> *To tell you the truth, I had not thought of it that way! But you're right. I suppose that's why I sought them out as readers—because they were influential. I imagined my readers to be the Brian Williams and Katie Courics of the world, knowing that if they read the site, then others would think they had to read the site, too.*

Did he have any idea that his blog would open so many doors for him?

> *No. I started the blog because I thought there wasn't enough coverage of cable news. I knew I could do it myself. I didn't know it would lead to job offers—though in retrospect I should have. The blog was a giant résumé, a giant "hire me" sign.*

Like Brian Stelter, Marcy Massura went "from blog to job" and didn't stop there. In addition to her blogging work, she's a vice president of digital at the communications agency MSLGROUP, an author, and a speaker. When I asked her how new bloggers can stand out in such a crowded field, she said:

> Be exceptional. Too many bloggers are busy being average, copying others, and working every angle possible to get brands and agencies to notice them. But the bloggers we agency people are interested in have well-written content, good photo and video skills, and have strong niche communities around specific topics and genres. Those bloggers are exceptional. Secondly, the ultimate key to blogging success is consistency. Be consistent in everything from your publishing schedule, your content quality, and your tone. Being great every once in awhile is interesting, but success is built on doing something consistently well.

Selfish Versus Self-Interested

After chronicling my "social job search," I found that what was resonating with people was a mix of guidance and motivation—something I didn't expect, given my *extreme* distaste for self-help books. But I ran with it, and it continued to work. This wasn't a formula or recipe—anyone who purports to possess a formula for "success" in any realm should be ignored. What I had found, however, were two truths that are as close to universal as truths get:

1. People are self-interested. This is reflected in their content consumption and sharing.
2. Content that benefits its consumers will ultimately benefit its creators and distributors.

With few exceptions, the people who get the most out of social media are the ones who consistently deliver something of value to their audience. The most popular homemade videos on YouTube make people laugh. Or they help people. I recall being surprised at the number of views—often in the hundreds of thousands—of the videos I would watch when learning to shave with a straight-blade razor. But should I have really been surprised? These videos solve problems that people have in their lives, no matter how small those problems may seem to an outsider. Sitting there with a face full of cuts and a new razor, I turned to these videos for help, as did hundreds of thousands with the same problem. In that moment, the problem loomed large, and the solution was in reach.

Why Do We Share?

If we consume content that helps us in some way, what motivates us to share it? A study by the *New York Times* and Latitude Research asked this question. The research found five general motivations for sharing, three of which are fundamentally self-interested:

1. We share to bring valuable and entertaining content to others (mostly altruistic).
2. We share to define ourselves to others and to receive social validation (mostly self-interested).
3. We share to strengthen and nourish our relationships with one another (mostly self-interested).
4. We share for self-fulfillment—"We enjoy getting credit for it" (mostly self-interested).
5. We share to advocate for causes we believe in and, less commonly, brands we want to support (mostly altruistic).[8]

The lesson here is simple: to become indispensable, become a source of content that fulfills as many of these motivations as possible, as thoroughly as possible. A few examples:

- @breakingnews has over 4 million Twitter followers because it provides news alerts before they become mainstream knowledge. It creates no original content of its own (besides the tweets), and it links to a wide array of sources.
- "Dad blogger" Ron Mattocks has earned high-profile speaking invitations, a book deal, guest columns, and media appearances, because his *Clark Kent's Lunchbox* blog helps other dads be better parents.[9]
- Ex-accountant Therese Schwenkler saw a profound need for a source of "nonsucky" advice for young people like herself, so she decided to create it. Her blog *The Unlost* is a source of inspiration and guidance for thousands, and along the way she's finding answers to her own questions.[10]
- Kate Spade New York realized that people wanted a "peek of what it's like to work at Kate Spade, and an inside look in the fashion industry," so the company made it the focus of its blog. "I think there are a lot of women that aspire to live interesting lives, and they can experience that in a very authentic way through our blog," says vice president of eCommerce Johanna Murphy.[11]

Audience First

Self-interest can mutate into selfishness when value is promised and not delivered. Or when people ask for things before they've provided much of anything themselves. Examples include "squeeze pages" that ask for personal information before any value is "dispensed," a Twitter stream that contains only self-promotion, or mass Facebook messages asking for votes from people the sender hasn't interacted with in months or years. These don't help anyone but the originator—there is no mutual benefit.

To be that indispensable person or company, it is essential to understand that our self-interest will be fulfilled only when we fulfill the self-interest of our audience first. Social media offers no true shortcuts, but it gives us a powerful set of tools for delivering and receiving value.

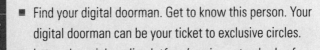

CHEAT SHEET

- Find your digital doorman. Get to know this person. Your digital doorman can be your ticket to exclusive circles.
- Let each social media platform's unique standards of reciprocity guide your outreach.
- Strive to become an indispensable resource to your target audience. Your content and engagement strategies should orbit around this central goal.
- People share things to bring value to others, make themselves look good, define themselves to others, advocate for things they believe in, and seek self-fulfillment. Make sure your content ticks one or more of these boxes.
- Put your audience first.

CHAPTER 5

From the Inside, Looking Out

Undercover Boss is a British television show with derivative versions in the United States, Australia, Norway, Germany, and Canada. The premise is simple: top corporate executives go "under cover" as low-level employees to "examine the inner workings of their companies." Filled with frontline revelations, tough lessons, and buckets of tears, the executives leave their adventures in the real world with a new understanding of the day-to-day realities of the people who keep their companies humming. There's something special about the show, as evidenced by the U.S. version's Emmy nomination and the fact that it ranked "as the biggest new series premier since 1987," according to CBS.[1]

The experience is often very humbling. The C-suiters routinely appear inept at performing simple tasks or seem clueless about things like how their products are actually made. But if we're to take them at their word, it's all worth it. Why?

There *are* indirect financial rewards for companies appearing on the show. Essentially, the companies profiled are getting free advertising during prime time to the tune of more than $12 million, as one estimate suggests.[2] Another analysis shows that many of the companies see a stock performance bump after appearing on the show.[3] But a lot of the "free advertising" is unflattering, and it seems unlikely that the share price spike is a safe enough bet for the TV appearance to be calculated for this potential benefit.

Inherent in the idea of access is some degree of vulnerability, which is one of the reasons gatekeepers exist. Those on the other side of the door can risk a lot by opening it—privacy, focus, efficiency, and more—so why do they ever do it? Being accessible, as it turns out, can be a winning proposition for the powerful, as well.

Escaping the Echo Chamber

Like Shakespeare's King Henry V, who donned a disguise to walk among his soldiers and get the unvarnished truth about their readiness for the next day's battle, many powerful people know that their "10,000-foot view" of reality is colored by career-minded yes-people, corporate groupthink, and their distance from the front lines.

The higher someone's status, the more other people say what they think the person wants to hear. When reality finally pierces the wall of optimism and flattery, it's often too late—this powerful individual has simply made too many decisions based on false premises to right the ship. As former Hewlett-Packard CEO Leo Apotheker told *Business Insider*:

> If you want to be successful, do not have only yes-people around you. Have people who will challenge you, have people with different opinions, and provoke a discussion.[4]

Getting continual access to these unvarnished opinions before they have been polished internally is now a matter of finding the social media side door. And more and more people are finding it, according to a study by Forrester, which determined that "eighty-six percent of business technology buyers engage in some form of social activity for work purposes."[5] In fact, another study by GlobalWebIndex found that business decision makers are likelier than the "average internet user" to engage in social activities like commenting on blogs, tweeting, and managing a social profile.[6]

An executive who knows how to navigate the social web is one who is willing to seek the truth, even if it yields some bruised egos in the C-suite.

Those who make important decisions based on a severely distorted reality will ultimately fail, so shrewd leaders place enormous importance on their back channels to the truth. This is reflected in the rise of internal social networks like Yammer and Salesforce Chatter, which can facilitate enterprisewide collaboration and that much-vaunted corporate "transparency." These networks serve, in part, to break down rigid silos and chains of command that can kill great ideas before they reach someone with the authority and resources to make them happen. On Chatter, for instance, a CEO can post a question to the organization and receive answers from employees from across the entire company at every level in the hierarchy. And yet at many corporations, a direct e-mail to the CEO concerning the same issue would be met with a layer of administrative scrutiny in the form of the CEO's executive assistant, at which time it may join a long queue of incoming messages, or it might die on the vine altogether.

It's worth noting, however, that employees don't have quite the same enthusiasm for the potential of these tools. According to a survey from Deloitte, "As it relates to management visibility, 38% of executives think social media allows for increased transparency while only 17% of employees agree."[7]

The Direct Line

I can't even fathom the anxiety Rupert Murdoch causes his PR people every time he tweets. Through this medium, the media billionaire speaks his mind with seemingly no restraint. Here he is giving what could easily be perceived as investment advice:

> *Markets right about Amazon, I think. eCommerce systems growing fast world wide. Big and small retailers in for very rough ride.*

Here's a political tweet:

> *We have to do something about gun controls. Police license okay for hunting rifle or pistol for anyone without crim or pscho record. No more*

And here's an informal legal defense:

> *@rathacat. Family agony awful, but caused by deleting voicemail and raising hope. NOTW wrongly accused of this by Guardian who corrected.*

It would be easy to dismiss these messages as mere rants, and perhaps they are. But what is remarkable about them is just how little they are scripted, manicured, and spun. This is a billionaire talking directly to whoever will give him their attention, without minders, legal departments, or copyeditors reviewing any of it.

And that's often the point behind proactive use of social media by leaders. There's no need to buy airtime or radio spots, no need to gather a crowd, to tell the world exactly what you think. No need to send to legal or to have the board review it. There's no "prior restraint" keeping you back if it's not on message or doesn't follow your brand guidelines. But that doesn't mean most leaders using social media don't restrain themselves—they do, most of the time. Social media is the way to get the ear of the masses quickly.

Spillover

Now that mainstream media has "discovered" social media (just look at the ticker of tweets at the bottom of the screen of any prime-time reality show), and now that the news commonly uses social media as a source, social content reverberates onto the radar of even those who don't use social media. Edison Research's *The Social Habit* quantified the extent to which social media enters the consciousness of even nonusers of social media. According to the study, 43 percent "hear or read about tweets almost every day in the media," 93 percent of Americans over the age of 12 have heard of Twitter, but only 10 percent use or have a profile with the network. The study also found that 45 percent of Americans over the age of 12 have heard of Google+, and yet only 8 percent use it.

The well known and powerful will have thousands or even millions of waiting and willing followers, simply by virtue of their name recognition. Kobe Bryant had more than 100,000 followers before his first post on Chinese microblogging site Sina Weibo.[8] Seth Godin hasn't posted anything on Google+, but more than 100,000 people follow him anyway. I imagine that's quite the ego boost—the "cocked and loaded" platform. Just click "post" for instant attention.

Humanization

The Supreme Court's *Citizens United* ruling, which found that the First Amendment protects corporate political donations as "political speech," falls in line with the legal idea of "corporate personhood": that in some legal matters, corporations should be treated as people.[9] But outside the court, the average person doesn't accept the humanization or anthropomorphization of corporations, because, well, the idea is absurd. Businesses don't have feelings or worries or hopes. The most important way this is reflected is in our declining trust of advertising and brand messages. A fascinating Nielsen report describes the widening trust gap:

Nielsen's Global Trust in Advertising Survey of more than 28,000 Internet respondents in 56 countries shows that while nearly half of consumers around the world say they trust television (47%), magazine (47%) and newspaper ads (46%), confidence declined by 24 percent, 20 percent and 25 percent, respectively, between 2009 and 2011.

But the people who make up the corporation, including its leaders, can imbue it with human qualities that are hard to ignore and may make the corporation seem trustworthy. For example, consumers who "buy American" aren't doing so to help American corporations but to help their workers. And although people are highly distrustful of government, they don't wish ill on government employees as individuals. Organizations, then, can score points by putting their people in the spotlight. Social media is easily one of the best ways to do that.

In fact, it's strange to interact with nonhuman entities, isn't it? This is why we see the official Twitter accounts of corporate giants using a few different tactics to make their corporate social presences seem a little less . . . well . . . corporate. One of the most common is the signature within the tweet. This tells the followers just who at corporate HQ they're dealing with. Often the caret symbol (^) is employed for this purpose, as in this tech support tweet from @GoToMeeting:

@pat4017 Open our side panel, it's most likely minimized to a tab on the right. ^GD

That "^GD" means it came from Glen, a social support rep for the online meeting vendor.[10] Another common tactic is having a single, identifiable representative as the Twitter point of contact. The @ComcastCares handle was made "Internet famous" by Frank Eliason, who wrote the rules of social media customer service. As a customer service rep, Eliason started to use Twitter to proactively address customer needs. And as Shel Israel puts it, "The enterprise discovered that quality support on social networks could generate as much attention as poor support had already shown."[11] When you were interacting with @ComcastCares, you weren't dealing with Comcast, but with a friendly, helpful guy named Frank. Frank went on to help Citi do the same, and he tours the country speaking about his experience—which, in retrospect, seems like a no-brainer, but it was in fact truly innovative. Now Bill Gerth runs the Comcast account, and his photo and bio add the kind of personal, human touch that hadn't been seen in social media before Frank Eliason.

Senior executives, specifically, can have a big impact on company perception by engaging in social media. The BrandFog *CEO Social Media Survey* determined that "81% of respondents [employees of companies of all sizes] believe that CEOs who engage in social media are better equipped than their peers to lead companies in a web 2.0 world." The survey also found that 89 percent of respondents agreed that social CEOs "can build better connections" with customers, while 66 percent thought that social CEOs could do the same with investors. But here's the real genius of executive social media use:

> *When asked what benefits C-Suite engagement in social media can lead to, 78% cited Better Communication and 71% stated Improved Brand Image as the biggest positive benefits.[12]*

It's that clear communication and accessibility, combined with giving the brand a personality, that makes the brand more human.

"I Am Barack Obama, President of the United States—AMA"

On August 29, 2012, President Obama sat down for an Ask Me Anything session on the social news-sharing and commentary site Reddit. Ask Me Anything, or AMA, is a longstanding and popular

Reddit tradition, where people with interesting stories or perspectives (such as, "I saved a girl from drowning. She then sued me."), including celebrities, take questions posted by Reddit users and answer those they wish. Obama's AMA thread generated 5 million page views and crashed the site. While it was interesting to see which questions the president chose to answer, the thing that made the experience so special and fascinating is that the questions were submitted by people who otherwise had no special access to the nation's leader. The questions he answered ranged in topic from funding for space exploration to the White House's beer recipe. And although he avoided that vast majority of the questions, he no doubt saw many more than he answered, which is still more access than the average person ever gets to the president. He started the thread like this:

> Hey everybody—this is barack.
>
> Just finished a great rally in Charlottesville, and am looking forward to your questions. At the top, I do want to say that our thoughts and prayers are with folks who are dealing with Hurricane Isaac in the Gulf, and to let them know that we are going to be coordinating with state and local officials to make sure that we give families everything they need to recover.

Who knows if the experience influenced him or altered his views in even the slightest way? In all likelihood, it did not, but that wasn't the point: the real motivation for his participation was to humanize him further in a critical election year and to energize a base of voters largely inaccessible by traditional means. In these ways it was a smashing success. Like the Twitter Q&A earlier in 2012, in which the president tweeted answers to seven audience-posed questions (and provided "photo proof" of his direct involvement), this was *radical* in its transparency and degree of access to the most powerful person on Earth.[13]

No one, not even the proudest of Republicans, will deny this: President Obama's digital strategy in the fiercely fought campaign was an enormous differentiator with *real impact*—on the national conversation, media coverage, and, yes, voter turnout. Social media's reputation among the elite as the unimportant, parallel-universe of "slacktivism" may persist, but it does so at its skeptics' peril.

I asked Teddy Goff, who served as digital director for the Obama campaign, how the idea of access figured into the campaign. "This was the whole ball game for us," he said:

> *We knew that by serving our people well, giving them tools and resources, and making sure they had all the facts and message points they needed to go out and spread the word for us, we had the ability to reach almost literally everyone in the country—and to reach them more effectively than we as a campaign could, because people are broadly skeptical of political rhetoric and advertisement, but they trust their friends.*

"Three out of four heads of state, are at present on the social media site Twitter," according to global agency Digital Daya.[14] They're using the channel to deepen and extend access with a massive human audience to which the preferred form of interaction and information seeking is digital and social in nature. So many of the most relied-upon outreach techniques fall pathetically flat in today's connected universe. Robocalls, which in the United States can only target landline phones, won't be very effective in reaching the millennials generation: more than 40 percent of them have abandoned landlines for mobile only.[15]

Tweeting with the Dictator's Daughter

On the extreme opposite end of the political popularity spectrum is "the most hated person in Uzbekistan," Gulnara Karimova. Karimova is the daughter of the country's dictatorial leader, Islam Karimov. She is hated because of the contrast between the luxurious, seemingly carefree life she lives and the grinding poverty and oppression faced by the vast majority of Uzbeks. Journalist Natalia Antelava, after many failed attempts at securing an interview with the first daughter, was able to get her attention on Twitter. From the radio program *PRI's The World*:

> *It came around completely accidentally. I noticed her tweeting with the communications director of the International Crisis Group. I noticed that she was responding to his tweets, and he was asking her about torture in the Uzbek prisons, and seeing that unexpected dialog, I thought, "Well, I might as well tweet to her, too." So, I sent her a tweet, saying, "Since you're so communicative, could you let me back into Uzbekistan? I was deported without an explanation," referring to a quite recent deportation. Just last year, I went to Uzbekistan to do a story, and was not allowed into the country, spent 24 hours in the airport, and was put back on the plane. And to my great surprise, she replied, and back and forth it went. It was quite a long conversation. A lot of it was about, you know, how she's misunderstood, but then she said, "Sure, I can try to help you find out about what happened; send me all the details." And she sent me her email address, to which I sent her a letter.*[16]

But Karimova's promise was hollow. After receiving no reply via e-mail, no help whatsoever, Antelava wrote about the bizarre exchange in the *New Yorker*. Karimova was "quite upset" and accusatory and took to Twitter to confront the journalist. After resending the e-mail at Karimova's request, Antelava still hasn't received an answer. Commenting on Karimova's curious accessibility, Antelava said:

> *I think that her reputation bothers her, and she does want to fix it, although she doesn't know how. But again, I'm just speculating and guessing to be honest. But there's certainly some sort of*

insecurity and insensitivity that I sense through that conversation,
and the fact that she engaged in the first place is all part of that.

Everyone wants to be loved.

Listening Leadership

For as long as social media has been properly studied, theorists and researchers have noted the "1 percent rule," coined by Ben McConnell and Jackie Huba.[17] McConnell wrote that "roughly 1% of your site visitors will create content within a democratized community."

Jakob Nielsen refined the rule, categorizing users into three groups: those who "account for almost all the action" (1 percent), the "editors" or "intermittent contributors" who "contribute a little" (9 percent), and the "lurkers who never contribute" (90 percent).[18] One way to think about it is that one group is sending many original signals; another is receiving those signals, modifying them, and sending fewer signals altogether; and yet another group is only receiving the signals without sending any of their own back into the ecosystem.

Evidence like the *CEO.com Social CEO Report* suggests that the proportion of senior executives creating *any* social content is probably a lot lower than the 10 percent reflected in the general population.[19] In terms of adoption, 70.3 percent of Fortune 500 CEOs have no social presence. Looking at content creation reveals numbers like these: only 3.8 percent of Fortune 500 CEOs have joined Twitter, and half of them haven't tweeted in the last 100 days. But does that really make them inactive, as many commentators have suggested? Certainly, these CEOs are missing out on some of the benefits we've discussed earlier in this chapter, but it's likely that many of them are getting plenty of value out of simply "lurking." These leaders can research what their customers are posting about them and their companies without ever posting anything themselves by making use of a few simple searches or Google Alerts or by checking social media streams periodically. Behind many of many supposedly "inactive" profiles lies a more conservative—but still important—use of social media: strictly as an information source. If this knowledge is their only objective, public social activity is unnecessary.

Leaders can still be reached through social media *even if they don't personally use it at all.* This is another kind of spillover. A study I led for Bazaarvoice, in collaboration with the CMO Club, found that nearly 90 percent of chief marketing officers say that "social data has impacted at least some of their decisions." This is content and data that are pulled by others and reported to them, whether or not they have any personal social presence. And the social data doesn't stay with the CMO, either: the study showed that the data is being shared with sales teams, product management and development, HR and recruiting, and other executives within organizations (one in four do so weekly).[20] This means that access to even the most senior decision makers can be achieved by engaging with those around them and in other areas of their businesses.

Extending Influence

One of the more interesting dynamics in the social space is the ability of one's social presence to outshine the influence and notoriety one has in life "outside" social media. Stephen Fry, the English actor, writer, activist, and comedian, was not particularly famous beyond the United Kingdom, but he has amassed a global Twitter following of more than 5.7 million. His wit and way with words translate perfectly to Twitter, putting him on the radar of users who may not even be familiar with his body of work. The influence he wields has brought down countless websites, ignited a national political debate about New Zealand's technological infrastructure,[21] given an unexpected boost to the careers of musicians like Jon Gomm,[22] raised the profile and filled the coffers of many obscure but important charities, and provided what might be considered the best model for celebrity use of the social network. He ponders this influence on his blog:

> *Well, I shall level with you. It never started out as my intention, but the result of my life in Twitter is that I need never ever contribute to print media in any form again. Ever. If you have more followers than subscribe to the* Independent, Guardian, Times, Financial Times *and* Daily Telegraph *combined, then you can finally dispense once and for all with the whole horror of having to submit yourself for interview and profile.*[23]

Fry has used Twitter to promote himself and his passions directly to people, without having to willingly participate in the media circus. And his global influence on Twitter has far exceeded his global influence prior to his use of social media.

Forget the Intermediary

Shira Lazar is known as the creator and star of several web video series, including her flagship *What's Trending*, a hosted countdown of popular YouTube videos. The last time I ran into her, she was being shoulder-pressed by Shaq, live on camera from the Samsung Blogger Lounge at South by Southwest. She joined Twitter in 2008, and she has opened up some major social media side doors with celebrities and viral video stars through Twitter. In fact, rap star Talib Kweli appeared on the very first episode of *What's Trending* after the show's coexecutive producer sent him a tweet saying that he and Shira would love to have him on the show. "He then DM'd us his info to set up the interview," recalls Lazar. Social media also helps the show land interviews with rising stars before the major networks reach them.

I asked Shira what makes Twitter such a unique access channel to celebrities:

Twitter strips away the middleman. If a talent or personality wants to do something they'll do it. If you tweet them, they can check you or the brand out for themselves and judge the value and how relevant it is in a new way. Celebrities need to find innovative ways to connect and engage with their community and it's not necessarily through a press release or soundbites on the typical shows. Traditional celebs need to figure out ways to engage beyond the promotional cycle or else their brand will lose relevance. Fans want to know they're supporting someone that cares, not that is just trying to constantly sell them something. Audiences will care when they join you on your journey, not just on the good days when you have a TV premiere or movie release. That comes down to connecting with an individual—not a publicist or mouthpiece.

Much like actors and musicians, journalists, too, have seen their stars ascend as a result of active participation in social media. Their use of social media for information gathering far exceeds that of executives and other professionals, with 55 percent of journalists worldwide using social media content from known sources in their journalism and 26 percent doing the same with sources not previously known to them.[24] But they aren't just sitting back and taking notes, either. They're building their own personal brands, and they're often giving themselves exposure in markets beyond their daily newspaper or network subsidiary. And they're putting a human face on the news, just as executives are using social media to put a human face on corporations. In an interview with Sara Fidelibus of Poynter.org, social media expert Brittney Gilbert (who worked for NBC Bay Area at the time) put it this way:

People would much rather interact with NBC Bay Area's meteorologist or sports reporter than a faceless entity such as NBC.[25]

Safeguards and Sanity

Appearing accessible without making oneself too vulnerable is a modern balancing act—and in this case, being vulnerable means being exposed not just to dangerous activity but to anything that saps productivity or focus. Being barraged with private DMs on Twitter isn't fun, but it comes with the territory if you're a well-known user of Twitter who follows too many users back. In Stephen Fry's case, hundreds of users barrage him every day with DMs, in addition to thousands of mentions, "only the tiniest fraction of which I will get a chance to see, let alone directly answer."[26]

One safeguard, then, is to be very deliberate about the people you follow and friend and to "prune" them once the noise becomes louder than the signal. A Pew study found that 63 percent of Facebook users in 2011 had "unfriended" at least once, compared with 56 percent in 2009.[27] Facebook has noticed this trend and is now offering ways to "mute" and selectively group certain users, rather than unfriend them. The Pew study also revealed another trend toward clamping down on access to personal profiles. Only 20 percent of social networking users keep their most used profiles completely public, whereas 58 percent set their profiles to be viewed by friends only, and 19 percent maintain "partially private" profiles. A newer network called Path is one of the first in an array of social media options aimed at making the online social experience as intimate as the offline one. Or as Path CEO Dave Morin puts it, they're trying to create a home in the social web:

> *The information you naturally consume inside your home is quite different from most of the information you consume as you're walking down a city street. In your home, you're more yourself.[28]*

For high-profile users, communications security is appropriately paramount. In light of scandalous private message leaks and accidental public updates, many of these users will avoid private communications via social networks to minimize the risk of sensitive information winding up in the public sphere.

Ashton Kutcher made an interesting move by partially handing over management of his Twitter feed to his own agency after a gaffe related to the Penn State sex abuse scandal caused an uproar. His observations no doubt echo what many other notables are thinking:

> *It seems that today that twitter has grown into a mass publishing platform, where one's tweets quickly become news that is broadcast around the world and misinformation becomes volatile fodder for critics.*[29]

The way Kutcher described the role his agency, Katalyst, would play in his use of Twitter is interesting. The agency will serve "as a secondary editorial measure," or a form of gut-check oversight. This seems like an ideal model for someone who feels that his words can get him in trouble, yet values authenticity. As Kutcher writes in his blog post, "A collection of over 8 million followers is not to be taken for granted." The alternative, of course, is the "ghost tweeter."

For some celebrities, social media is a threat to what little privacy and control they have left. When I spoke with Jane Levy, star of the hit horror remake *Evil Dead* and *Suburgatory*, she told me she had abandoned Twitter three times already. "I understand its value, but I've concluded that I like my privacy," she said. She continued:

> *I feel like you can't ask the world for privacy if you have a Twitter Facebook profile. I spend too much time on the internet anyway, and I feel like social media—especially Twitter—is fundamentally narcissistic . . . and too much responsibility.*
>
> *Once I started to get followers, I freaked out. I didn't want it anymore. I didn't want to be defined by whatever it said on this stupid profile. Every time I posted something, I felt funny about it. I was constantly deleting stuff I wrote. I didn't want people knowing about my personal stuff. And I deleted it.*

In exchange for her privacy, Jane may be sacrificing at least some of her appeal as an actress. She said, "My publicist just told me recently that when two actors are fighting for a role, how many followers each has on Twitter is a big factor."

Social Ghosts

Ghost tweeting probably began as soon as the notable and powerful joined Twitter, but it's impossible to know for sure. Most ghost tweeters are publicists, PR people, agency folks, and the like. It makes sense. Busy people with little time to master something pay others to get the results they want through the age-old art of "sanctioned impersonation." Ghosting runs the gamut from obviously fake and outsourced to impossible to distinguish. What is true of ghost tweeting is true of ghostwriting, too—the people who hire ghostwriters can be very involved, up to and including outlining the piece for someone else to draft, or they can be completely removed from the process, simply signing off on content before it goes public; but sometimes they don't even take this step. Author Mark Schaefer recounts a conversation he had with a friend who was trying to open up her own side door to the C-suite:

> I have a friend who had been building a Twitter relationship with a business executive she admired. They had tweeted back and forth a few times and he had provided some helpful career advice to her. When they had a chance to finally meet at a networking event, she introduced herself and was met with a puzzled stare. He had never heard of her before, and sheepishly explained that his PR agency was tweeting for him. Obviously his reputation was ruined for this young woman . . . and also . . . all those she talked to about the incident![30]

Data on the outsourcing of personal social media accounts is scarce, but by looking at the huge increase in the use of social media for corporate accounts (a 128 percent bump from 2010 to 2012), we can safely assume that "personal outsourcing" is going up as well.[31] If brands can do it, why not personal brands? It seems the potential for inauthenticity of voice is trumped by the upside of time savings, risk aversion, and consistency. This usually spells a loss for those trying to access the client, as third parties are yet one more hurdle to direct communication. They may not share the interests of the client (you may find yourself thinking, "I'll bet the *real* Ashton Kutcher would follow me back"), or they may even be instructed to serve as a bulwark to access. Either way, they are gatekeepers to be reckoned with.

Signing Off and Sharing Too Much

Other leaders and celebrities abandon social networks altogether, when the risk and distraction become too difficult to deal with by tweaking settings and avoiding private messages. The list of "Twitter quitters" includes Alec Baldwin, Charlie Sheen, James Franco, and many more (although celebrities tend to "rebound"—such is the allure of unfettered access!).[32]

Greek track and field athlete Voula Papachristou learned the real-world consequences of unbridled tweeting when she let a racist joke slip and was dismissed from the Olympic team by the Greek Olympic Committee.[33]

Another athlete, pro tennis player Rebecca Marino, has decided to quit tennis, in part because of social media's damage to her mental well-being. The 22-year-old Vancouver-based player, who has ranked up to thirty-eighth worldwide in the Women's Tennis Association, has battled depression for six years. Cyberbullying via social media, she told reporters, "has taken its toll on me." Interestingly, Marino was "warned" by Tennis Canada about Twitter's risks when she decided to open an account, "but they also thought the shy girl might benefit from a chance to open up and express herself online." Along with professional tennis, she's leaving Facebook and Twitter.[34, 35]

Singer LeAnn Rimes was so affected by the incessant "torrent of abuse" that she subjected herself to by being active on social media, she checked into a rehab "to learn and develop coping mechanisms."[36] And yet Rimes still tweets several times daily. After rehab, Rimes told the *Boston Herald*:

> *I think it's really hard to deal with Twitter and Facebook and all these social media outlets. And it's hard to take it day after day of reading and seeing things that someone you don't even know says about you. As much as you said you don't want it to penetrate, it does, because you're human.*[37]

Sometimes, public figures open up way more than they intended to on Twitter. Lance Armstrong tweeted his own cell phone number, which was then retweeted almost 3,000 times.[38]

Silicon Valley venture capitalist Dave McClure was the victim of his own "DMfail" when a private message about a scandal he was involved in ended up in his public feed. It was a nasty one, too:

> *Ron is throwing us under a bus. and it's chickenshit that he writes that after David Lee comes to both meetings.*[39]

If McClure had only a few hundred followers, the mistake would have probably gone unnoticed. But the tech titan had close to 100,000, and not all of them, apparently, are willing to look the other way. The tweet was soon archived, retweeted, and posted to other networks, leaving McClure exposed. Clearly a Silicon Valley investor like McClure isn't technologically inept—the guy knows his way around a social network and advanced devices. But as with all social networks, we are forced to use interfaces that we didn't create, which means the probability of human error is high.

The most powerful DM fail in history took down a U.S. congressman. After he posted a photo of his crotch to Twitter, Anthony Weiner told reporters that he "intended to send [it] as a direct message as part of a joke to a woman in Seattle," and then he lied repeatedly about it by claiming he had been "hacked."[40]

Things shared intentionally can spark massive public backlash and have major consequences, as well. Gwyneth Paltrow was buried with criticism after tweeting "Ni**as in paris for real," even though she used asterisks and was referencing a Jay-Z song, as she later argued in her defense. Spike Lee retweeted what he thought was the home address of George Zimmerman, the man who killed Trayvon Martin, and had to pay a settlement to the actual residents of that address.[41] Rapper Bow Wow glorified his own drunk driving by tweeting twice in the same night about being "tipsy as f*ck" and driving his "lambo."[42]

Social Networks: Not Ours

All this stems from something that must be understood about social networks: they are not ours. Data ownership issues abound, since users are passing information through systems they did not build and do not own. Facebook has admitted that it monitors chats for criminal activity, prompting questions about what else it monitors. Twitter and Facebook divulge user information and content in response to court orders and subpoenas from law enforcement agencies, and both are susceptible to malicious exploits like phishing and malware. But even if all our activities are aboveboard, we are subject to terms and conditions we didn't write (and let's face it—we didn't read, either), structures we didn't build, and rules we have little power to change. Most use social media platforms for free, so it's hardly fair for users to expect 100 percent obedience to their demands.

People enjoy being where their friends are, even if this means opening the door a bit and trading their privacy for community. While this seems like a vulnerability, it's also an opportunity for people with good intentions to slip through the opening and engage with them—to join the community that they opened the door for in the first place.

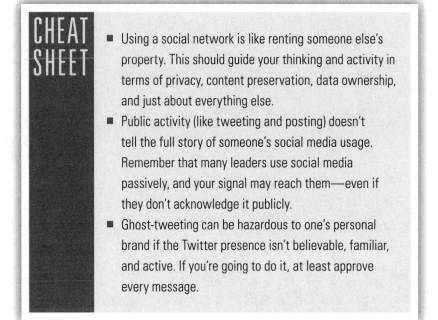

CHEAT SHEET

- Using a social network is like renting someone else's property. This should guide your thinking and activity in terms of privacy, content preservation, data ownership, and just about everything else.
- Public activity (like tweeting and posting) doesn't tell the full story of someone's social media usage. Remember that many leaders use social media passively, and your signal may reach them—even if they don't acknowledge it publicly.
- Ghost-tweeting can be hazardous to one's personal brand if the Twitter presence isn't believable, familiar, and active. If you're going to do it, at least approve every message.

CHAPTER 6

Egomania

Sir Ray Tindle will have none of your mourning for the death of his industry, thank you very much. His Tindle Group owns 230 newspapers, remains successful, and has been doing something positively shocking by today's standards: launching *new* papers—including 7 in London alone in 2012. Tindle Group hasn't found a new model so much as remained faithful to an old one, the hyperlocal paper.[1] "No cat should have kittens in Tenby without us knowing about it," he advised the *Tenby Observer* newsroom in 1978, redrawing the Welsh paper's scope of coverage to go no farther than Tenby proper. From his perspective as the ever-rare newspaper mogul whose ventures are still thriving, the formula for success is simple: "local names, faces, and places."[2] People still buy papers, in other words, when coverage reflects *them* and their immediate surroundings. And when Tindle papers print news items submitted by the community, they see sales increase.[3] Although relevance plays its role, the secret force behind the Tindle model is ego. Not Sir Ray's. The readers'. It's remarkable how well this lesson translates to the world of social media.

The quickest way onto someone's radar is through his or her ego, to reimagine that old phrase about the connection between heart and stomach. We like to surround ourselves with people who make us feel good about ourselves. Hollywood stars have their entourages, but those of us a bit closer to Earth start relationships with people that reinforce our self-image. There's nothing inherently bad about having an ego and doing things in service of it (as I've written elsewhere, "The concept of ego really gets a bum rap").[4] Whenever we praise and compliment, bestow awards and recognition, quote, link to, retweet, or even merely follow someone, we are dealing with a person's ego, intentionally or otherwise. But appealing to another's ego can be a perfectly tasteful and legitimate way of advancing our own interests. Consider the following two requests:

1. "Could you meet me for an hour each week to discuss my career trajectory, give me expert advice when I need it, and serve as a reference when I'm looking for a new job?"
2. "I'm really inspired by your success, and I'd love to follow in your footsteps. I'd be honored if you would act as my mentor and work with me to help me shine, too. It should take no more than an hour a week."

Most people would be more likely to accept the second request, because it paints the same activities as an extension of their personal success, instead of a request for work with no pay, which is the way a cynic might describe it. This concept applies incredibly well to the world of social media.

Ask First?

Sometimes, the best way to start a relationship with someone who has hardly noticed you yet is to ask for something . . . small. The perfect access-granting request is for something that is low effort for the people being asked and of significant value to you, and . . .

- Makes them *feel good* about themselves
- Makes them *look good* to others
- Is public facing
- Helps them, even in a small way, get more of what they're after (like publicity)

Not all these conditions need to be met to make the request successful. A lot of it depends on the context—how familiar are people with you or your work, and how do they view themselves? All the conditions above offer *ego capital*, which is the element that makes something appeal to the ego. Almost anything can be made more powerful with the help of ego capital: marketing, sales, job searches, even relationships. There's an important distinction between ego capital and flattery. One of the more common definitions of flattery is "insincere or excessive praise," in other words something that is over the top by its very nature.[5] (That's the definition evident in the famous idiom, "Flattery will get you nowhere.") Ego capital may harness the same dynamics, but it can be used in a tasteful, genuine manner—unlike its flamboyant cousin, flattery. Flattery is ego capital gone wild.

Participation Chains

Small requests can lead to deeper, more rewarding relationships. For example, I've always been amazed by this study, which we summarized in a Bazaarvoice report:

> *As part of a consumer research study, residents of Dallas, Texas, received a phone call asking if they would let a Hunger Relief Committee representative come to their homes and sell them cookies, with the proceeds to be used to buy meals for the needy. Only 18 percent agreed. But, when the caller started by asking, "How are you feeling this evening?" and waited for a reply,*

32 percent—nearly double the earlier number—agreed to a visit
from the cookie seller. Even more astounding was the fact that
once someone followed up by paying a visit, nearly everyone
(89 percent) made a cookie purchase.[6]

The authors of the paper, former Bazaarvoice CMO Sam Decker and advisor Ze Frank, call this phenomenon "the participation chain." Every interaction makes the next one flow more naturally. A small request that is granted makes a subsequent larger request more likely to be granted. In my experience, this is absolutely true. If people give me a quote for a piece I'm working on, I know I've got a better shot at asking them for a full interview in the future. If I've conducted that full interview with them, I can probably manage to secure an in-person meeting with them when I'm in town. Most of this participation chain is not calculated step-by-step; it occurs naturally over the course of any relationship. But the continued acceptance of my requests is reliant on the experience they had fulfilling the last request. For example, whether they say yes or no to an interview for my blog is going to be largely contingent on whether the post I quoted them in previous blogs was well received by readers, whether it gave them enough exposure, or whether it gave them the affirmation—that bit of ego capital that *everyone* wants— that they're after. If so, they can expect an even greater return on their next investment of time and mental energy with me, and I can expect them to say yes to my next request. Look for ways to inject ego capital into every step of the participation chain without turning it into a flattery chain.

The Interview Model

Who doesn't want to be interviewed? When someone asks you to do an interview, it makes you feel "interview-worthy." And you have more control over the content in an interview than any other format—the piece centers on *your* words. If you, the interviewer, make it as easy as possible on the interviewee and provide evidence that you can really get the piece out there, in front of an audience that the person cares about, you have a great shot at a successful request. It's also important to help promote something that the interviewee is specifically trying to promote, like a new book or a special event.

Often, when people who influence me release a new book, I reach out to them for a simple e-mailed back-and-forth interview. I reference the interviews I have done in the past with people they no doubt admire themselves—people like Seth Godin, Guy Kawasaki, and Brian Solis. It feels great to be in company like that! If they agree to the interview, and the vast majority of these authors do, I'll ask them questions about their book and point a few links in their direction. It's amazing the level of author you can get when they have new projects to promote.

The interview posts generate an incredible amount of traffic, because the authors promote them on their networks as social proof and as exposure for their work. These are people I want to interview for a few reasons. The first is to extend and deepen our relationship. The second is to reach and influence their audience. When this second goal is met, web analytics data shows me that the traffic the person sends to the post is staying longer, hailing from my target geographies, and engaging and sharing more than other visitors. If not, I still have a great piece of content that my existing readers will enjoy and a better relationship with this person.

If I were looking for a job again today, one of the first things I'd do is send blog interview requests to top executives at companies on my list. Executives love talking about their accomplishments, and while I might have to circumnavigate a few skeptical public relations managers, I know I'd get through to at least a few of the top brass. An interview would serve as social proof for both the executive and me, and the interview process would open up a social media side door that I could later capitalize on for job-hunting purposes. And even if the project didn't *directly* get me a job, I would have a powerful new node in my network of influence, an interesting blog post, and a possible reference.

Interviews with corporate leaders are sometimes "vanity opportunities," in that the interviews have strong ego appeal and tend to make the executives look good while providing little actual value to their organizations, except for those difficult-to-quantify benefits of thought leadership and awareness. The term *vanity opportunities* is derived from Chris Dixon's "vanity milestone," which he defines as "achievements that are more about making you feel good than helping your company."[7] The most blatant example of a vanity milestone I've encountered was at the popular Dreamforce conference, where all the marketing materials for one of the new vendors focused almost exclusively on the founder's serial entrepreneur legacy, the amount of capital he had raised, and the names of Silicon Valley stars who had invested in this company. What did the company actually do? None of the other attendees seemed to know . . . or care.

Finding a direct approach to the executives through social media or another means (like a powerful second-degree contact) is important. If you go through their company's communications or PR unit, your request for an interview may be vetoed for lack of wider organizational benefit before it even gets to your would-be interviewee. This is true of any opportunity involving ego capital: the more gatekeepers you have to muscle through to get to whom you want, the more your attempts will be diluted and ineffective. If you must take an indirect route, your best bet is finding a way to position the request to all the members of the chain so that they all find value in it. If, for example, you're dealing with PR handlers first, you might promise to touch on key corporate messages in the interview. If you're asking a contact for an introduction, you might offer a special callout link in your post to thank the person for connecting you. Gatekeepers have egos and aspirations just like the rest of us, and doors often open because you have something to offer the gatekeepers and not just those they are guarding.

Connecting Social Proof and Ego

As noted in an earlier chapter, social proof is the heuristic (mental shortcut) that tells us to make choices based on the choices of others. Even people at the top want to provide more social proof of their accomplishments. What kind of social proof they're after can take any number of forms. They may be trying to reach a specific number of outlets, so they can make a statement like, "as quoted on over 100 blogs." Or they might simply be after network growth, in which case a good interview and a link to their social profiles will do the trick. Almost anything you do to provide social proof will *also* appeal to their ego. It's a powerful double whammy that can lead to an amazing degree of access.

As an example, I worked on a video profile series about leaders in social media and disruptive innovators. I made a list of the people I wanted to interview and sent out introductions that detailed why I was approaching them specifically and how the videos would be promoted and used. The response I received was extremely positive—and honestly quite surprising. Many of these people have made multiple appearances on national television; they've all been written up in tier-one press; they charge in the tens of thousands for speaking appearances. But they like the idea of having another professionally produced video in their collection of social proof, especially one that focuses on their biggest accomplishments and asks them for their expert opinions. They are able to embed the video on their website, add it to their reel, and otherwise hold it up as proof that they are true thought leaders. I'd be a fool to impose restrictions that would limit their ability to self-promote in this way—no one would agree to do the videos if they were solely to be used on *our* website, for *our* purposes. Any time you can empower people with a social proof boost and a simultaneous ego stroke, you're making it almost irresistible for them to agree.

Is there anything wrong with finding a mutually beneficial way to make someone feel good, in pursuit of something greater (like an excellent blog post)? Not if you're going for substance over flattery.

Earlier in the book, I talked about a study by the *New York Times* and Latitude Research. Recall that three of the five general motivations for sharing content were "fundamentally self-interested": to define ourselves to others, to strengthen and nourish our relationships with one another, and to receive self-fulfillment.[8] If the ego motivates so much of our sharing behavior, what else does it motivate in the digital realm?

Egosurfing the Pingbacks

A Pew Internet study found that "more than half (57%) of adult internet users say they have used a search engine to look up their name," a phenomenon known as "ego surfing" or "vanity searching." Not surprisingly, this number is on the rise, likely due to increasing web savvy, rather than ego inflation. This leads us to one tried-and-true method of getting people's attention: writing about them. With the scope of search expanding as Google and Bing compete to index and display social content within results, a name within a public tweet, Facebook update, or blog post is fully searchable. So when the stars align and you're writing about a topic that is ripe for a quote from people you'd love to know better, seize the opportunity to include a quote by them.

But there's no need to sit back and wait for the itch of their ego to compel a bit of ego surfing. Send the item to them, tweet it to them, etc. Let them know you appreciated their quote so much, you had to include it in your post. Pingbacks from links and Google Alerts accomplish the same task here, and often simultaneously. For example, if you quote people from their blog and link back to the source, there's a good chance that they'll get a Google Alert for their name and a pingback for the link and that they will also find your post during their next ego-surfing session. What happens next largely depends on the quality of your work. They might contact you with a note of thanks, bookmark your post, share it, or subscribe to your blog. Or they might do nothing at all, in which case, you still have a great blog post to your name. One of the pleasures of being a blogger is speaking with people you admire and being surprised when they tell you they are familiar with your work—or better yet—a fan. Maybe they would never have found your blog if you hadn't mentioned them in that post.

Not So Subtle

I can recall one time when I played the ego angle too obviously, and it backfired on me (ironically, the title of my blog began with "Social self-importance").[9] I was eager to get another post up on my personal blog, and I really wanted inbound links from bloggers I admired. Plus they had (and still have) huge networks that can drive waves of traffic with a single tweet. I was obsessed with the idea of content curation at the time and was writing a lot about it, so I decided I'd try to kill two birds with one stone: I'd write a post on a topic that had been a crowd favorite before, and I'd try to put myself on the radar of some of the top bloggers in the universe. The post itself, in which I curated some quotes about curation—very meta!—wasn't the issue; it wasn't just thrown together like a lot of the list posts you'll see out there that are strictly designed to stroke the egos of everyone on them. For my burgeoning blog it got decent traffic. Amber Naslund, one of the influencers I quoted, even tweeted it and then dropped by to leave a great comment. But I got greedy. I wanted more! I had quoted Brian Clark (of Copyblogger.com notoriety), so why wasn't he doing the same? After all, I had tweeted a message telling him I had quoted him, I had sent him a note about the post through his site's contact form, and I'm sure he received a Google Alert and a pingback alert as well. A day later, still puzzled, I shot out another tweet, reminding him of the post. His reply has since been lost in the ether, but it was curt—something like, "Yeah, I saw it." At the time, I didn't understand why he would be so rude. But later I realized that he wasn't being rude at all. *I* was the rude one, because I was acting like I was entitled to something from him that I had no right to expect. He had probably been approached by 10 others that day, just like me, trying in some way to play into his self-importance. There's also a chance he didn't care for the post he was quoted in, so expecting him to promote it was presumptuous at the very least. Like so much else in social media, reciprocity is not assured.

This experience exposed me to some simple truths about ego capital and side doors. First, there is no formula out there for the successful use of ego in outreach. Second, the ego card shouldn't be used so openly, or it can seem entitled, calculated, or even desperate. Third, everything you do to work the ego angle should *also* create value in another way (if it's content, the content should be great even if your ego strategy doesn't work out).

Social Currency

Social currency is defined by Vivaldi Partners as "the extent to which people share the brand or information about the brand with others as part of their everyday social lives."[10] So how can we create things that, when shared by others, pass on a little of our brand as well? The answer lies in the ego, as it so often does. Something that offers ego capital is more shareable than something that does not. And something that offers ego capital *and* social proof is irresistibly shareable.

Take blog badges, for example. Blog badges are the little images that identify blogs and bloggers as part of an exclusive circle or as having won or accomplished something prestigious. The Ad Age Power 150 badge, for instance, is a popular badge among top marketing bloggers because it signals to their visitors that they are high up on a list of some of the most popular blogs in the world. Ad Age created a few good-looking, easily embeddable versions of it and released it for free. It gives these bloggers social proof and also a nice ego boost. The master stroke of the badge is the fact that it carries the Ad Age Power 150 branding and is hyperlinked by default back to the Power 150 web page. By embedding the badge on their blogs, bloggers are also sharing the Ad Age Power 150 brand with their massive audiences. That's social currency at work.

The social influence measurement platform Klout is deeply infused with ego capital. It creates social currency by giving users information about their status and making it effortless for them to share this status information with their networks. For example, if I'm looking at my Klout score, I am prompted to share it. The auto-filled tweet is the perfect mix of ego capital and social currency, in that it shares both *my* brand and the Klout brand simultaneously.

> *My Klout Score is 64. Join me on Klout to discover yours today:*
> *klout.com/user/be3d?n=tw&v=daily_welcome&i=68634*

When Klout users claim perks (brand-furnished rewards triggered by their influence in certain areas), the site prompts them to "Share your excitement about this perk." In fact, almost every ego-fulfilling view and action can be easily shared, including lists of people influenced by the user.

Location-based check-in service Foursquare has mastered this dynamic as well; as I've described it on my blog, every public check-in shares a bit of the Foursquare brand:

> *People are way more inclined to share where they are when that*
> *location elevates their social status. Just having a structured, fun*
> *way to brag a little about that exclusive concert or referral-only*
> *New York cocktail club turns our physical location into ego capital.*
> *Imagine, for instance, the simple thrill of checking into the TED*
> *conference for the first time.[11]*

Try asking people to share something positive about you, and you're making a request. But give people a way to share something positive about them? That's a gift. Putting others first in your content means that, when shared, it will contain less social currency (more about them and less about you). But it also means the likelihood of being shared is many times higher, which means a larger amount of social currency overall is being passed on to social networks.

Intel's Museum of Me is as clear a demonstration of this truth as you're likely to find anywhere. Visitors to the site log in with their Facebook accounts and watch as a sentimental, aesthetically interesting "visual archive" of their time on Facebook is played. Users happily share their journeys with others, who in turn create their own Museum of Me. Imagine if the experience was called Museum of Intel and all the content was Intel-related. Except for a tiny contingent of hard-core Intel brand advocates, no one would share it.

The "Good-Company Approach"

During South by Southwest Interactive 2012, a contact at IBM reached out to secure an interview with me for a web series that IBM was filming on-site at the convention center. I had a conflict during the time of the shoot, so I was going to have to respectfully decline. I called my contact, and before I had the chance to break the news, she asked me if I had had a chance to see the other interviews in the series, and in particular, the one with Tim Berners-Lee. I stammered, "Like, the inventor of the *Internet*? *That* Tim Berners-Lee?" She laughed and gently corrected me, "He invented the World Wide Web, but close enough." There was no way I could turn this opportunity down now! Whether she had done it intentionally or not, this person had appealed to that part of the ego that tells us to measure our own success, in part, by those we are associated with. It's the same social proof lens we use to evaluate the external world, used as a mirror instead. Of course I don't think I deserve to be in even the same *sentence* as Tim Berners-Lee, but being in the same video series made me feel great, and I had to accept the offer.

Once you've opened a side door with individuals who are recognizable and esteemed, make sure to create a "public record" of it whenever you can (and always with their permission). This can be a quote from them, a reference, an interview, a photo of their participation with you in an event (like a conference panel), or anything else you can show in order to signal to others that if they engage with you, they will be in good company. Businesses leverage this same principle when they show their "NASCAR slide" with the logos of their most recognizable clients during a pitch to a prospect. Sometimes the good-company approach is aspirational: they want to be like the others you provide as social proof, and you are positioning yourself as a step in that journey. Other times the good-company approach is a matter of providing qualifications: people want to make sure you can play in their league. It all depends on whom you're approaching and how they view themselves within their space.

Exclusivity

The more exclusive you can make a request, the more ego capital it will contain. In the video example earlier in this section, IBM's request would have been less appealing if I knew it had asked 200 others to shoot a video as well. This dilution of ego capital would happen for two reasons. First, it would have simply made me feel less special; I would have shared the stage with 199 others, instead of just a handful. Second, my name would have less *proximity* and a weaker connection to the great Tim Berners-Lee. Think of it like a party: if the person you're inviting knows that the guest list is being carefully planned and is limited to a small group of interesting or well-known people, that person will be more likely to attend than if it were an open invitation.

Every few weeks, I'm invited by a company to its Twitter chat, and in each invitation, the company mentions my name and reminds me of the time and topic. If I found that the company was churning out hundreds of these invites to people I've never heard of, I probably wouldn't attend. But I have checked the company's tweets, and I've determined that the company actually seems very deliberate and thoughtful about the people it invites, and I recognize many of them as people I respect and even admire. I've participated a few times now, and I admit that my decision was largely based on the ability of the company to combine three things into one invite: ego capital, exclusivity, and the good-company approach.

Companies Have Egos, Too

In my job as a business-to-business marketer, access is the name of the game. It's what everyone's after at first. Our job is to create great content that gets people to engage with us, or it's to create that "positive familiarity" that warms up the call from the salesperson. We're going for that moment of recognition: "Oh yeah, I know you guys. You put out that video about the future of the Facebook-enabled toaster oven. Sure, let's talk." Or something like that. The same forces are at work with business-to-consumer companies, too, except the familiarity is geared to influence the moment of a consumer's decision, whether online or in the aisles. One of the best ways to gain access to prospects is to write about their industry and challenges and to mention their companies in the content. It's a strange thing to say, but *companies have egos, too*. This angle shouldn't be used wantonly, nor should it be used in every piece of content you put out, but it does work when the tactic is used in a way that doesn't alienate the rest of your audience for the sake of that single prospect. It also works well with existing clients.

A few years ago, I attended a conference in Las Vegas. It was the first conference I had been to while working for Bazaarvoice, and I went, in part, to prove to my then boss that conferences could help generate great content that would have an impact on the business. Normally, we'd only send salespeople or product marketers with deep knowledge of the technical side of our products (not a content guy like me). In retrospect, I'm a little embarrassed about how little I knew about what Bazaarvoice *actually did* at that point, but for some reason I didn't think I would be put on the spot about it.

When I arrived, I saw that one of our clients was presenting. This was a multibillion-dollar Fortune 500 company, and yet our relationship with the client wasn't very mature yet—that's marketing speak for "the client isn't using many of our products, and we aren't getting paid very much (relative to the client company's market cap)." Fortunately, the topic was interesting to me, and I thought it would be interesting to our blog's readers as well. I sat anonymously in the audience and took notes. I didn't know the presenters, and I didn't have time to introduce myself before the next session.

Later that week, back in Austin, I posted a recap of that session to our blog. I had a few back-to-back meetings, and when I got back to my desk, I saw that Bazaarvoice had been mentioned a few hundred times on Twitter in the space of two hours (this doesn't happen often). The tweets were from employees and divisions of the company whose session I wrote about. That alone may have been enough to secure me a ticket to the next conference of my choice in the eyes of my boss. Then I checked the traffic to the post. Through the roof—more traffic that day than any I could recall seeing, ever.

A new e-mail notification popped up on my screen, from the salesperson at Bazaarvoice assigned to the account. He had forwarded me a thread that was sent to him by his internal champion at the client company. It showed the extent to which the post I had written had wound its way through some of the highest levels of this organization. People there were proud that their colleagues had done so well in their presentation, and it made the company look really progressive. The last message in the thread was a note from our internal champion to our salesperson, thanking us for the coverage and asking if the two of them could set up a meeting soon to talk about expanding the relationship.

This event-recap model worked wonders for us again, a few times. After a Facebook executive spoke at our annual conference, I wrote a post about the ideas within his talk. I never directly sent him the link, but within a few hours of publication, our web servers were being pushed to their limits. Facebook, which humorously has a Twitter account with over 5 million followers, tweeted the post. It was one of the highest traffic days in Bazaarvoice history.

A Matter of Pride

Pride. If you write something that *you* can be proud of and that portrays prospects or clients in a way that *they* can be proud of, you've found a way in or secured a foothold from which to dig deeper. The next step they take with you may be motivated by ego (they want more) or reciprocity (they want to do you a favor in return), but you won't know, and it doesn't matter which it is anyway.

Ego is a funny thing. We all have it; so many of our thoughts and actions are prompted by it—and yet most of us learn to take great pains to hide it. Ego has always motivated humans to take steps toward a better life, and nothing about that has changed.

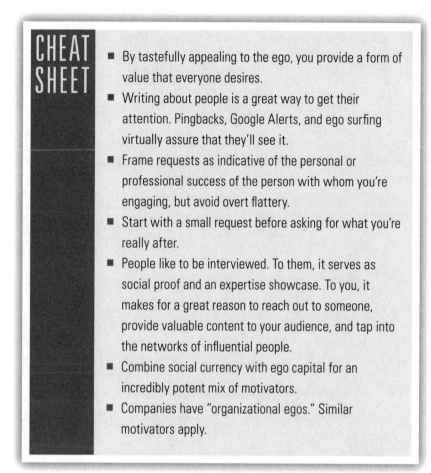

CHEAT SHEET

- By tastefully appealing to the ego, you provide a form of value that everyone desires.
- Writing about people is a great way to get their attention. Pingbacks, Google Alerts, and ego surfing virtually assure that they'll see it.
- Frame requests as indicative of the personal or professional success of the person with whom you're engaging, but avoid overt flattery.
- Start with a small request before asking for what you're really after.
- People like to be interviewed. To them, it serves as social proof and an expertise showcase. To you, it makes for a great reason to reach out to someone, provide valuable content to your audience, and tap into the networks of influential people.
- Combine social currency with ego capital for an incredibly potent mix of motivators.
- Companies have "organizational egos." Similar motivators apply.

CHAPTER 7

Access, Influence, and the Social-Industrial Revolution

What follows is an October 2012 Twitter exchange between Edward Barr, a *Wall Street Journal* subscriber, and Rupert Murdoch, billionaire media mogul:

Edward Barr: @rupertmurdoch second time in one month no WSJ at my door. In today's world that is beyond inexcusable#especially@$438peryear

Rupert Murdoch: @esbarr_ Yes. Where are you?

Edward Barr: Lexington, KY 40502, a great product that I miss when not there on timely basis#thanksforthepromptreply

Rupert Murdoch: @esbarr_ thanks. If you don't hear from customer service in 24 hours tweet me again.

Barr is not a social influencer. He had 54 followers in 2012. Murdoch is a household name, followed on Twitter by upward of 370,000 people, and the man behind a vast media empire. The *Journal* is just one of dozens of newspapers owned by Murdoch's News Corporation. Murdoch is one of the few Twitter users who could actually *buy* Twitter. Why would someone like this respond to a single subscriber's customer service issue? Because individual consumers have more influence now than ever before in the midst of the Social-Industrial Revolution.

No Sidelines

What we're living through right now is a revolution of choice, access, and influence: the Social-Industrial Revolution. It's an era of consumers and businesses rethinking and redefining their roles and relation to one another. Consumers finally have knowledge, choice, visibility, collective voice, and individual influence. This fresh empowerment doesn't come at the expense of all businesses, but it will absolutely threaten those who refuse to see it as an opportunity. There are no sidelines in this revolution, no safe vantage points. Everyone is a participant, and we all stand to gain.

Neglecting the needs of consumers wasn't always bad business. Consumers didn't have many choices, and what choices they did have were difficult to evaluate and exercise. The default option won, not because it fully addressed the demands of consumers, but because it was the best option within reach. Consumers are still used to waiting in call center queues for bad service, products, and services that underwhelm them. They take for granted that companies value shareholders over customers, and they have come to expect poor experiences, confusing terms of service, PR spin, and ad bombardment. But for the first time in the history of commerce, consumers have options. And offering consumers exactly what they want, at scale, is starting to make sense to businesses.

Economic disruption produces both winners and losers (and usually more of the latter). In the first and second Industrial Revolutions, entrepreneurs like Richard Arkwright and Henry Ford successfully detected and adapted to the winds of change. Firms that couldn't, or wouldn't, adapt were forced out of business. The first true middle class emerged. Millions lost their livelihoods, and millions more entered the workforce to meet the labor necessities of mass production. Consumers got cheaper, lower-quality products. A mixed bag, if ever there was one. The balance of power between businesses and consumers shifted decidedly in businesses' favor, and there the scales remained, practically motionless, until very recently.

The End of Assumptions

This is an era of data visibility—where access to information levels the playing field, opens up a universe of choice, and lowers barriers to entry for both consumers and businesses. As consumers access more sources of information and entertainment, and as they engage with other consumers and brands on sites like Facebook, businesses are learning about them through their data.

And access is often a two-way street. While this raises many legitimate privacy concerns, consumer data has tremendous potential to benefit not just businesses, but consumers themselves. We've arrived at the "end of assumptions," where the abundance of consumer data means guessing is no longer necessary. Businesses know, or can know, exactly what the market wants by analyzing social media, search, web, financial, demographic, and psychographic data. They can make more things, to meet a wider array of needs, at less risk and more profit. Social data is like an alternative energy source, because the data is a form of a familiar "raw material," word of mouth. Like water or wind as energy sources, social data's potential is unlocked as we discover new and better ways to extract value from the raw stuff. *Not knowing* is the first cardinal sin of the

Social-Industrial Revolution—as we'll explore when we talk about adaptations; *not acting* is the second.

Many consumers are beginning to see their data as an asset, not just a threat to their privacy when exposed. Several projects like Personal are involved in creating a marketplace for users to voluntarily exchange their own data for various forms of value. But because consumers give so much of their data to sites like Facebook at no charge, companies aren't lining up yet to buy what they are used to obtaining for free from social networks and ad services. For more on what this marketplace might look like, I recommend reading *The Intention Economy* by Doc Searls.

Connected Perspectives

Mobile devices seamlessly connect consumers to people and businesses and to the premarketing truth about the things they might purchase. They address blind spots in communication and information that have historically placed people who are on the move or are in remote locations at a disadvantage. Mobile devices are shrinking in size while packing in more computing power and utility than the average consumer knows what to do with. We're integrating this technology into everyday objects like smart refrigerators, shoes that track our steps, and cars that provide us with personalized, real-time information and entertainment. And we're stringing them together over wireless networks so that the devices talk to each other, upload and download data to and from the cloud, and make our lives more intuitive and user friendly. Shoppers use apps like RedLaser to engage in price comparison and read reviews while standing in the physical aisles.

Businesses, too, are reaping tremendous benefits from mobile technologies. Employees now have handheld knowledge centers that can eliminate communication and data siloes, providing access and visibility into every corner of their companies. Even container ships at sea now enjoy mobile coverage.

Whom Do You Trust?

Consumers have escaped the channels that marketers built for them. Before the Internet and social media, if we wanted information about a product before purchasing it or about a company before doing business with it (or working for it), our options were severely limited. If our friends and family had no experience with what we were considering and if journalists weren't covering it, then we used print, TV, in-store, and radio ads to fill in the rest. In other words, marketers accessed consumers while consumers accessed content. Businesses were able to minimize the extent to which off-brand and unflattering messages reached consumers. They owned or rented almost all the real estate in the media landscape, and they perfected the art of wooing a captive consumer audience. The Internet, social media, and smart mobile devices gave consumers new avenues of access to information. Reality began to intrude on the space previously occupied by squeaky-clean marketing facades—consumers were talking to each other, finding alternatives to overpriced or ineffective products, pouring sunlight on business practices that were previously hidden. They began to trust the opinions of total strangers more than the words of advertisers. Some consumer cohorts, like the millennials (generation Y), began to trust total strangers *more than their own friends and family.*[1] Consumers today can choose where and how to access information and communicate. One's immediate circle rarely holds all the answers, and for the first time ever, it is easy to find answers outside that circle. Not all the information is accurate; much of the content shared and created lacks substance or is plainly offensive; many consumer complaints are unfounded. But as a whole, we see consumers exercising options that are themselves new—as if all around the world, we're discovering new superpowers and we're excitedly learning to use them. People being born today are digital and social natives, but perhaps more important, they are the first fully empowered generation of consumers. What will they do with their new superpowers, with their newfound access and influence? We're just beginning to find out, and luckily for those of us who study this kind of thing and businesses that are looking for new avenues to growth, the results are constantly coming in, billions of data points at a time. Charles Angoff said, "History is a symphony of echoes heard and unheard." The present and future are symphonies of data.

Consumer, Inventor, Designer, Promoter, Investor

Every link in the supply chain is being disrupted, reshaped, and improved. Consumers are helping companies decide which products to stock. Walmart's Get on the Shelf program was a successful experiment in product assortment: consumers voted on crowd-submitted products, deciding which ones would end up in select Walmart stores. Start-up site Quirky takes the "inventing together" idea quite a bit further. Every week, 10 user-submitted ideas are subject to design, market, and viability testing, with site members involved at every step. The top two inventions are put into development, and then users participate in every aspect: pricing, product naming, and more. Finished products can be purchased from Quirky or from select retail partners such as Staples, Target, and Amazon.

Crowd funding on sites like Kickstarter is creating micromarkets for products that would otherwise never make it into production due to production costs, lack of capital, and awareness gaps. Crowd-funded equity allows ordinary consumers to be micro angel investors who put their money in start-ups, and instead of receiving cool swag or early dibs on a product, they will get an actual stake in the company they support. New language in the 2012 JOBS Act makes this practice possible for the first time in U.S. history. Just as Southwest Airlines made air travel accessible to the average U.S. consumer, venture capitalism is being made radically accessible as well. When customers are also part owners, so one theory goes, they'll make better, more even-handed decisions. Group buying models like Groupon are allowing consumers to use scale to obtain better pricing and unique offers that individual consumers would never see. "Presumers," a term coined by Trendwatching .com, describes the growing segment of consumers who "love to get involved with, push, fund, and promote products and services before they are realized."[2]

Rapid prototyping, powered by 3-D printing, makes product design and iteration far cheaper than the inefficient and costly subtractive prototyping models that have been the standard since the first Industrial Revolution. The *Economist,* as usual, sees the future:

> *No longer does a producer have to make thousands, or hundreds of thousands, of items to recover his fixed costs. In a world where economies of scale do not matter anymore, mass-manufacturing identical items may not be necessary or appropriate, especially as 3D printing allows for a great deal of customisation.*[3]

The top manufacturer in the 3-D printing space, MakerBot, makes machines that can literally print their own replacement parts. Thingiverse is the first of what will surely be a flood of sites that allow consumers to print objects at home from user-uploaded designs; brands will join the action in the near future, once they work out how to approach the complicated intellectual property angle of this new consumer-facing technology. If consumers have access to print-at-home alternatives to your products, why do they need your brand, and why on earth would they visit a retailer to buy it? We're not quite there yet—materials and print quality aren't yet mature enough to print, say, a pair of Nikes—but we're not too far off, either.

Consumers are even innovating on their own time and at their own expense, before and after purchasing products. An MIT study found that "millions of citizens innovate to create and modify consumer products to better fit their needs." In the United States alone, for instance, 11.7 million consumers are either creating or modifying consumer products to the extent that the money they spend doing so is equal to 33 percent of "companies' R&D expenditures on consumer products," and the average U.S. consumer-innovator spends the equivalent of 9.9 days of his or her own time every year engaged in this kind of innovation.[4]

Your Platform Awaits

Platforms used to be large, unwieldy things. They took years to build, piece by piece, and millions to buy and rent. Audiences were not free to acquire. Just think about a single TV ad. A brand pays an ad agency to create the ad, and the agency pays the broadcaster to air it in a particular time slot. In that time slot airs a show that the broadcaster has invested millions to produce and build an audience for—all at a tremendous risk of failure. And for hundreds of thousands or millions of dollars, the brand is paying for the right to 30 seconds of that audience's time. All things considered, this was still a pretty sweet deal when that audience was captive, before TiVo, the web, and social media. Traditional models like this are still used because, as much as new media wonks like myself hate to admit it, they still work well enough for most brands. But alternative platforms can now be built at a fraction of the cost, and sometimes they even emerge organically or unexpectedly.

Certainly, one tweet was a big enough platform to allow Edward Barr to reach Rupert Murdoch. Definitely an anomaly. But we can easily imagine two other probable outcomes of Barr's tweet. The first is simple: nothing. Millions of tweets are lost in the noise or ignored every day. Indeed, a normal billionaire probably wouldn't do a thing about one customer's concern. Imagine if Bill Gates responded to every Windows complaint or if Richard Branson took to Virgin America's Facebook wall to address upset travelers—not going to happen (consistently, at least).

The second outcome is the social snowball. Other *Wall Street Journal* subscribers in Kentucky, nationally, or globally could have seen Barr's tweet, retweeted it, or chimed in with their own concerns. The snowball would gather speed and size until *someone* from the *Journal* addressed it. Maybe it would get local media coverage—"Kentucky *WSJ* Subscribers Not Getting What They Paid For"—and then show up in the Google Alert of a PR manager, who would delegate a local response and solution. It's almost a joke how easy it is to imagine that scenario! In fact, the customer service odyssey of Ken and Meredith Williams followed roughly this trajectory. After hitting roadblock after roadblock attempting to get through the front door of Bank of America while trying to buy their first home, being unable to reach people who could help them, and being ignored across all traditional means of communication, they found a side door: they parodied their own situation in a musical YouTube video called *Close This Loan!* The video features calls to action for viewers to take to Twitter and visit a no-frills WordPress blog that outlined their plight. According to CNN, "Local news outlets picked up the couple's story and within 48 hours, the bank got in touch."[5] Just four days after posting the song on YouTube, the loan was closed. On their blog, they give a nod to "those Bank of America employees—especially ^ek at the Social Media Services team for her quick response and follow up on our claims."[6]

Today's consumers also have access to audiences through the ready-made dynamic platforms that other people and organizations have built. The power one wields just by leaving a comment on a large company's blog is completely unprecedented. Even a single comment can literally change a website, leaving its imprint for the company and other consumers to see. Companies hope that most of that user-generated content will be positive, but they realize it won't always be praise. The worst thing they can do is appear to facilitate public feedback while censoring negative content in an attempt to bias public perception, because consumers will take their grievances elsewhere, armed with a new, more powerful complaint: their voice is being suppressed. Savvy consumers will find a platform until someone with power hears their grievance and responds to their satisfaction.

Public shaming works wonders. I had a recurring issue with my car stereo's auxiliary audio jack while it was under warranty, and I took it to the dealership, which claimed it wasn't the jack; it was the cord I was using to connect to my iPhone. Naively, I believed the people at the dealership—until the situation became unbearable and the stereo simply wouldn't play audio from an external device. I found other consumers with the identical problem on several forums. At that point, my manufacturer's warranty had expired, so I called the brand to plead for an extension or free repair. No dice. I described the issue on the company's Facebook page. Nothing—the manufacturer was overwhelmed with similar such complaints and didn't respond to all of them. Then I remembered that the dealer that claimed the issue was my fault had (of course!) a Facebook page. I copied and pasted my grievance from the brand's page to the dealer's page, and I left my phone number. Less than an hour later, someone at the dealership called to offer me a free repair. What did the dealer want in return? You guessed it: take down the post. I suggested instead that the transparent thing to do would be for me to update the post with the fact that I was being taken care of, and the person I was talking to agreed. The lesson? If you're getting nowhere, find the place where you can leave the biggest, most public blemish simply by telling the truth. Smart companies won't leave it there unaddressed for long.

The *Consumerist* is the blog offshoot of *Consumer Reports* that puts a modern spin on its parent organization's remit, which is to fight for "a fair, just, and safe marketplace for all consumers and to empower consumers to protect themselves." It's the perfect third-party ally, and it's expert in helping consumers get access and resolution, to the chagrin of the thousands of companies that have been the focus of the *Consumerist*'s public shamings. Once a consumer complaint is covered on the blog, resolution can happen in a matter of hours, as when DirectTV responded to a post about sporadic TiVo service, took ownership of the issue, and agreed to compensate affected sub-scribers.[7] Not surprisingly, the issue was first noted in hundreds of comments on a customer's thread on TiVo's own forum that began 11 days before the story made the *Consumerist*.

America's Next Top Influencer

During one my more colorful phases, I took to smoking an old-fashioned tobacco pipe (maybe it made me feel more like a writer). The problem was, packing a pipe that stays lit for more than a few minutes is more difficult than it looks. I could have driven the mile and a half back to the tobacconist and sheepishly asked him how to actually make use of the tobacco he sold me, but stubborn pride prevented me. Naturally, I took my query to the web. On YouTube I found hundreds of videos, giving me *exactly* what I was after. I sorted by popularity and went through the top three at my own pace (all were in the hundreds of thousands of views), positively over the moon that I was able to learn this way instead of having to request the tutelage of the grizzled tobacconist in front of all the good ol' boys who hung around the shop. The guys in the videos used different brands of tobacco, and either they talked about why they favored their brand, or the tin labels were clearly in the shot. After combining some of the finer points of all three pipe-packing methods, I visited the tobacconist again and bought several of the brands featured in the videos that helped me most. These video stars weren't compensated by the brands they featured, and it's doubtful that they even received the products for free. They were just sharing what they knew—and what they liked—in a way that helped hundreds of thousands of people who were just starting to develop habits and brand loyalties that may stick for life. I still wonder, how many tins of tobacco were sold as a direct result of these homemade videos? And do these brands have any idea about the videos and what they've done for their brands?

The democratization of influence, along with the falling costs of audience acquisition, can work in companies' favor. Social media has created an army of citizen influencers—otherwise normal individuals who wield huge social footprints and outsized influence. They discuss and review films, music, products, and everything else under the sun. They have earned the uncompensated attention of thousands of subscribers, fans, and followers who tune in *by choice*—not because they have no other choice. Advertisers have traditionally measured their ads' effectiveness, in part, by how many sets of eyeballs they reached. But eyeballs that are there because they want to be there—interested eyeballs—are much more valuable. Consumers don't need any prodding to tell each other what they're buying, using, and wanting to buy. Brands are a big part of how people view themselves and how people want others to view them.

But while all consumers, to some degree, see the brands they purchase as a reflection of who they are, millennials take this association to another level entirely. Edelman Digital found that millennials are likelier to share brand preference online than any other personal identifier—including religion and race.[8] This generation *feels* empowered, too. The same study reveals a strong sense of self-importance unique to the millennials: "We also found that 76 percent of Millennials think they are highly depended on for their opinions."

I'd be remiss not to mention the "mom blogger" phenomenon here, since it crystallized the value of consumer influencers to the PR and marketing professionals who were responsible for building brand buzz. The consumer packaged goods industry, fiercely competitive and expert in the science of consumer choice, saw an opportunity to eke out a few additional points of brand preference in a familiar way—product giveaways. In these bloggers they found a digital version of the very Tupperware parties they invented, but with a vastly wider audience.

The model has since expanded into the broader practice of "influencer relations," with every industry trying to find its own version of the storied mom bloggers. There aren't any industrywide standards for doing so, which can work to your advantage. Normally,

PR agencies are hired by brands to find and engage with supposed topic influencers, but in my experience, their targeting isn't exactly laserlike. On one occasion, an American car manufacturer invited a friend of mine to a sneak peek of the Austin auto show and a gathering at an upscale restaurant, and he brought me along. My friend and I do not blog about cars, nor did anyone else at the event (at least to my knowledge). That seemed strange; there are plenty of auto bloggers in Texas. Maybe, I thought, this brand is on to something—trying to get nongearheads with local influence to generate some interest in their presence at the show, widening their scope. A month or so later, the same friend was flown out to Las Vegas by the same auto brand's agency. He didn't blog about it, and he didn't even tweet much about the trip. It seemed that he was a known quantity to the agency, the people there liked him personally, and they paid for his trip because they had a seat to fill. Sometimes it's that simple.

On another memorably puzzling occasion, I was invited by a PR agency, on behalf of a smartphone brand, to be a VIP guest at a party during a conference. When I got to the venue, I skipped the line and was given a gift bag at the door that included the latest-model smartphone from the brand that sponsored the party, worth a few hundred bucks. I don't blog or tweet about smartphones, or even electronics. I have exactly zero influence in those categories. I can only guess that someone at the agency recognized my name from something else and—once again—had a VIP seat to fill. Getting your name out there can yield unexpected returns.

Now They Want More

While influencer discovery practices are often rudimentary, the ways that brands and their agencies work with influencers are beginning to mature. Just as consumers are becoming aware of the value of their own data, so-called influencers are starting to understand their value to brands. Ask any marketer or PR pro with experience in this type of outreach if it's more difficult today to curry the favor of social influencers than it was two years ago, and you're likely to hear a story about upped antes and new layers of gatekeepers who prescreen requests. New agencies are springing up to represent bloggers, much as literary and booking agents represent authors and speakers, and more traditional agencies are diversifying into this lucrative new client base. An agency named Sway Group has been created specifically to act as representatives for influential bloggers, serving as an agentlike intermediary between brands and "nearly 60 high influence bloggers in a number of content verticals with combined monthly page views of 25 million." Nowhere is this more apparent than in the world of fashion, forever the realm of the glamorous trendsetter. From a *New York Times* piece about the rise of agency-represented fashion bloggers:

> *Until recently, fashion bloggers were paid with free merchandise, if they were paid at all. But that started to change as their influence grew. Now fashion bloggers are "right up there with editors in helping to mold what the consumer is going to buy," said Alexis Borges, director of Next Model Management, an international modeling agency.*[9]

But the influencer marketplace is like any other with low entrance costs: it will become extremely competitive. Brands that don't want to pay soaring premiums for the services of established influencers will focus instead on working on those with emerging platforms. This makes the relationship more participatory. Instead of piggybacking on someone else's platform, brands can help build a newcomer's platform. For example, an amateur auto photographer has excellent photos but a limited distribution network. Brands can help her get that reach, in exchange for commissioned work of the brand's models. American Express OPEN Forum is another interesting model in this vein. The small-business-themed content hub features the work of experts who write about all areas of entrepreneurship and strategy. Drawing nearly 330,000 unique visitors a month, it offers an enormous amount of exposure, 85 to 90 percent of which arrives organically (i.e., not via ads).[10, 11] Urban Outfitters identifies promising "street fashion" bloggers, seeds products for them to promote in their own unique voices, features the bloggers modeling the clothes on the Urban Outfitters' website and blog, and promotes the bloggers in e-mail campaigns.[12]

Marshall Kirkpatrick is one of the thinkers who shape the way I view influence. As the former coeditor and lead writer at *ReadWriteWeb*, he wasn't afraid to challenge some of the hollow metrics that supposedly establish social influence, and he identified more than a few that *should* be part of the conversation. Kirkpatrick left *RWW* to found the start-up LittleBird, one of the more exciting and useful influencer discovery tools on the market. I asked him for his perspective on the value of emerging influencers, and I really like his answer:

> *Identifying emerging influencers provides a unique competitive advantage; it's an investment in the future. Just like any speculative venture, engagement with thought leaders who are still emerging in a market offers outsized gains when it works. Relationships you develop now can grow into ones where you as a brand are the first to learn about ideas that emerge from the people on the edge of a network, where you can act first and have the most authentic relationship with a thought leader in the future.*
>
> *Just like in any other field, those who find great resources first are in a position of strength. In social media, those resources are people. When I was working as a journalist, key sources I discovered early and engaged with helped me to break news stories before my competition. Working in marketing, PR, Business Intelligence or other research fields, anyone can swim up the river of news and engage with innovators and influencers before their competitors.*

Small businesses are also reaping the enormous benefits of democratized influence. I spoke with Bonnie Joy Dewkett, a professional organizer who has seen her platform (and business) grow at an astonishing rate. She noted:

> *I was approached by* Better Homes and Gardens *to take part in their annual organization issue. It was the first time I was quoted in a national publication and I asked how they found me. I had previously tried to pitch them many times but was never able to "get through" to anyone. I was told they found me via Twitter and liked the content I was providing and that's why they called. Five years ago it was necessary to hunt down the contact information of each media outlet and try to contact them with a pitch. Now it's easy to make oneself known to TV outlets, print outlets, etc. Simply put a notice out and many will reply. Or they can find the type of person they are looking for by searching social media.*

Misty Young, who runs a four-location family restaurant chain in California and Nevada, recalled to me the moment when she realized that all her work building digital influence for the chain was about to pay off:

> *We were using all of these tools with some success when, out of the clear blue sky in November 2009 I got a telephone call that started innocuously enough, with, "Would you mind talking with me about omelets a little bit?" After a very energetic hour-long conversation, the woman on the other end of the phone tells me, "Well, the truth is, I'm a producer for the Food Network, and my job is to find people and stories that I think would translate well to television. And I think I found one!" After I peeled myself up off of the floor, I asked her, "how did you find us?" And she said, "We troll the Internet, we listen to what people are saying, and then we do our own research!" That process—started completely in the*

social space—ended with my company and myself being featured on the Food Network's Throwdown with Bobby Flay.

Food Network's spotlight shone good fortune onto Misty's chain, Squeeze In. Revenues shot up 25 percent the very next day after the show aired, and the cash injection carried over to the next year, funding two brand-new locations. "I'd say that's been a pretty good return on investment from something that started out as simple playing in the social media space," she told me. "Frankly, I'm completely stoked. We really pay attention to our brand, our work on it, and our engagement. We're just regular people who 'get it.'"

What I find really refreshing about the Squeeze In story is that the indicators that matter (revenue, new locations, awareness) tell the real story, not the numbers that a lot of social media strategists obsess over: followers, fans, subscribers, and the like.

Tracy Vega, who cofounded a self-defense training academy for women, explained to me how she used social media to join the *Ricki Lake Show*'s viewer community and earned massive exposure. After being selected as the show's "Friend of the Week," Tracy was invited to cohost the official #FriendsofRicki Twitter chat on the topic of self-defense. Her business also received coverage on the show's blog and garnered her an appearance on the "After Ricki" uStream chat. "We wanted to be involved, and we have developed a great relationship with several producers and their social media staff," says Tracy.

Even the biggest traditional media stage in the world, the Super Bowl, isn't the impenetrable old-guard fortress we might imagine. In 2013, Doritos gave average fans the chance to "Crash the Super Bowl" by submitting their homemade Doritos ad to a public vote. The two winners were given 30 seconds of access to the ultimate platform, when their ads ran during the Super Bowl. If their ads had been "awarded one of the top 3 spots" in the USA Today Ad Meter rankings, they would have received a cash prize of $1 million (number one spot), $600,000 (number two), or $400,000 (number three). Neither made it, but the Grand Prize winner, Mark Freiburger, won a chance to work for director Michael Bay on *Transformers 4*.[13] A 30-second spot in the 2013 Super Bowl cost approximately $4 million, up $500,000 from 2012, and yielded over a hundred million viewers. The show also has an abnormally loyal viewership by today's standards: In 2012, "only seven out of every 1,000 viewers turned the station during Super Bowl commercial breaks," which is "five times lower than the normal 'tune away' rate for commercials aired during normal TV programming," according to Jon Swallen, chief research officer with Kantar Media.[14] No, this isn't unfettered access; winners can't make or say whatever they want. It still has to be a Doritos ad, after all. But this model is exciting because, aside from the huge numbers associated with every Super Bowl, it's an innovative example of a formula we'll be seeing a lot more of: give consumers a vote in who gets the chance to use your platform. Second-place winner Ben Callner, director of "Goat 4 Sale," sums it up:

> *I think the fact that Doritos has a competition like this, where people like myself get a chance at the big stage is amazing. I mean, I think it's just the coolest thing in the world, and it's just kind of encouraging to everybody, that you can do it, you can compete with the big dogs. You know, if you've got a good enough idea, you can compete.*[15]

Times of crisis expose the real power behind the new platforms. Hurricane Sandy showed us both sides of that coin. The dark side was best represented by a single, despicably behaved individual: Shashank Tripathi. Tripathi used a pseudonymous Twitter account, @comfortablysmug, to spread intentionally fabricated misinformation about Sandy's impact. This update was retweeted more than 600 times:

> *BREAKING: Confirmed flooding on NYSE [New York Stock Exchange]. The trading floor is flooded under more than 3 feet of water.*

This one received 63 retweets:

BREAKING: Con Edison has begun shutting down ALL power in Manhattan

. . . which forced Con Edison to respond, as if it weren't busy enough trying to keep New Yorkers warm and safe:

@ComfortablySmug Info about shutting electrical service is wrong. #ConEd MAY shut service if low-lying areas flood

But "Hurricane Sandy's Worst Twitter Villain" faced serious consequences after he was publicly outed by BuzzFeed, not as a teenager in his mother's basement, but as a successful stock analyst and influential political campaign manager.[16] In addition to the de rigueur massive public shaming, he was threatened with prosecution and resigned (a.k.a. quit before being fired) from the state congressional campaign of Republican Christopher Wight. Needless to say, his written and tweeted apology fell deservedly flat with the people of New York and New Jersey.[17]

Add up every tweet from a trolling villain like Tripathi, all the doctored sharks-in-Manhattan photos, and every other bit of misinformation, and it's a tiny sliver compared with the positive effects of social media on the communities that lived through the storm, not the least of which was the capacity of social media to set the record straight and distribute accurate information to those who needed it most. As John Herrman observed, "Twitter's capacity to spread false information is more than canceled out by its savage self-correction."[18] It has been estimated that 8 to 20 percent of crisis-related tweets "provide situational awareness," which means that, on the conservative end, 40,000 tweets in the first three days of Sandy were potentially useful to relief and emergency efforts. Even with the proliferation of 24-hour news channels, traditional media's ability to distribute contextual, relevant information doesn't even come close to the power of social media.[19] And while the old media elite would like to knock social media for a perceived lack of accuracy (and its real lack of standards), let's remember that both CNN and Fox News got the Supreme Court's 2012 healthcare decision unfathomably wrong.

And so during the hurricane, as phone lines jammed (10,000 calls per hour in Manhattan alone) and other normal means of access to government entities were disrupted, social media became a lifeline.[20] Residents shared critical information with their networks as official sources struggled to reach and respond to them. Donations poured in through Facebook pages. Total strangers exchanged messages of support and solidarity. This was a community online, not an online community—and it benefited *real people* in a tough situation.

Adaptation

The name of the game for the business end of the revolution is adaptation. Companies must adapt first to the fact that they have, or have access to, accurate information about consumers that previously would have not existed (like a digital record of consumers' interests); or if information did exist, it would have been a mix of highly anecdotal, unreliable, and costly data (like focus group findings and telephone surveys). More important, companies must adapt to the fact that there's nowhere to hide. Bad PR, too many negative reviews, poor products, executives run amok, a not-so-green track record—there's no sweeping any of it under the rug for long these days. People will find out eventually, and they won't be happy when they do. The best marketing is making good products and delivering fantastic experiences. It wasn't always that way, but the days when marketing and PR could serve as the *antidote* to bad products are over.

Businesses are used to winning customers by pursuing one or more of a few standard differentiators. Cheaper, closer, bigger, first, and best—nail any one of them, and you would have a competitive advantage.

Globalized production and Amazon have made doing it cheaper nearly impossible. Retailers are losing a race to the bottom with Amazon, which can go much lower than traditional chains. Consumers used to equate "closer" with "convenient," but proximity as an advantage is losing its luster, fast—what's more convenient than shopping in your underwear and having it delivered to your office the next day?

Bigger was an advantage because, among other reasons, it meant reach in the form of advertising and the power to constantly stay in front of the consumer. As this chapter explores, that's not the case anymore. Being first meant you could quickly capture market share, brand awareness, and supply while the competition slowly ramped up. But barriers to entry in almost every industry are plummeting, and competitors are springing up from scratch and bringing new products to market as less agile firms lose first-mover advantage.

What's left? Best. Best will always be an advantage, and more so than ever before. When you are the best today, the connected world knows about it. Great products and experiences are recommended, reviewed, shared, blogged about, and bragged about. Consumers weren't always able to choose best, but they can now. Best is now more accessible, affordable, visible, trustworthy, and desirable. But getting to best isn't easy.

Best is data driven. Consumer data is often collected in the shadows, and it's not clear to consumers how sharing their data can actually benefit them. Smart companies are *asking* consumers for data access, building transparent systems in which that exchange can take place, and giving consumers a return on the data they collect. Consumers will naturally select those that offer the clearest and most compelling return on their data. Posh.ly is one of those companies. It's a website that specializes in cosmetic product giveaways by matching users with products and brands based on data from profiles that users continually update with additional data about things like skin type, complexion, allergies, and more. Cosmetic brands work with Posh.ly because they want to generate buzz about new products, but blanket giveaways are unreliable and wasteful; Posh .ly allows them to target the right product to the right consumer. In exchange for volunteering their data, users get great products, perfectly matched to their needs—for free.

Best is agile. Access to the bounty of consumer data and opinions is only valuable insofar as it leads to real change, and this process needs to happen rapidly in the Social-Industrial Revolution. This means that traditionally walled-off business units need to communicate in real time. It's now just as important for product development and marketing teams to have access to customer feedback as it is for customer service teams to have it. Agility allows companies to try new things, assess them as they happen, and optimize based on gathered signals and detected trends. Supply chains need to be transformed from linear pathways to visibility-and-collaboration loops, with all points in the ecosystem sharing relevant, timely data with the other stakeholders: design, production, supply, point of sale, end users. This new model isn't just more efficient; it makes everyone more accountable. In short, agility is what it takes to keep up with the new speed of consumption, communication, and decision making.

Accessing Your Brand

There is no end in sight to rising consumer expectations. Meeting and beating them is the challenge of this era. We're living through a truly unique spot in history. What you make matters more than what you say about it and how much you pay to say it. And you're making more than what's inside the box. Your product is the entire experience—from idea to design to creation to awareness to purchase and beyond—because that's what consumers now buy and share. They buy the ideas surrounding your product (e.g., TOMS' donating a pair of shoes "to a person in need" for every pair sold). They buy membership in a tribe (e.g., Harley-Davidson owners). They buy symbolism (e.g., the Louis Vuitton logo as a status symbol). They buy the *entire experience.*

Ever seen an unboxing video? It captures the experience of opening up something new. Unboxing videos are popular not because viewers don't know what's inside the box—that information can be found easily—but because people want to see and feel what it's like to own the product; they want to take part in the unboxing experience. They share *in it,* and then, of course, they *share it.* This is why Apple spends millions on developing and testing packaging, going through hundreds of prototypes of things like the adhesive pull tab on the iPod box.[21] It's also a part of the reason that Apple has put so little into developing a corporate social media presence; its presence lives in the countless posts per day from users celebrating their experience with the brand.

Ownership, physical proximity, and advertising were once the only ways for consumers to experience a brand. But consumers can now access a lot of the brand experience without buying, holding, or seeing the product on TV. They can test-drive actual cars by playing a video game, or they can try on clothes virtually. They can peek behind the curtain and see what it's like to work at Kate Spade by reading the employee blog. They can read and watch reviews and engage with customers on Twitter and Facebook. A lot of this is aspirational, like watching YouTube videos about cars you can't yet afford (I do this more than I'd like to admit). Other times, it's exploratory, as when consumers hit product forums looking for the right item for their particular needs. The act of purchase has been transformed from one of the only ways to access a product or brand experience, to the last step to unlock the "full" experience. In other words, a "product" is not just a physical thing but also a set of experiences, and buying is what consumers do when they want the fullest, deepest set of experiences available. Physical ownership, then, no longer has a monopoly on experience.

What you're selling is full access, or the fullest access feasible—the "complete" brand experience. Anyone can watch Taylor Swift's videos on YouTube or hear her songs on the radio; her album *Red* sold 1.2 million units in one week because people are willing to pay for the full Taylor Swift experience, and they want it as soon as possible. Her albums sell, at $14 each, because people want early and "exclusive" access.[22] On Target.com, the Taylor Swift store is promoted as "get more Taylor." Each retailer offers a different version of the album. The sellers compete by offering unique exclusive bonus content, like additional songs and remixes. But most revealing is the version she sells on her own site, which includes, among other things, "a special note from Taylor."

Alas, you're not Taylor Swift. Her brand is practically planetary. You sell auto parts, or software, or something else not nearly as exciting (don't we all?). It doesn't matter; you're still in the experience business. From the moment consumers become aware of a brand, across every encounter with it, to the research they conduct to make the right choice, to the point of purchase, the customer service interactions, the marketing e-mails they get from the company, and so on, they are accessing some aspect of the brand. They are comparing their experience with your brand with that of your competition, or what they know of it. You might make money on mufflers or software licenses, but what you make, what you sell, what people share with one another, is an experience.

The ledger analogy that I used in an earlier chapter to describe human relationships is useful in the brand-consumer context as well. Every point of contact between a brand and a consumer is an entry on the ledger, and the entries in the positive, neutral, and negative columns are constantly weighed against each other in the consumer's mental ledger. No Wi-Fi in your store for someone who wants it? No reviews on your site? Mark down two entries in the negative column. Responsive, friendly customer service via Twitter? That goes in the positive column. This tally runs in the background, but it's pulled up and referenced every time a decision is made.

Consumers compare your "score" on that experiential ledger with their other options: Should I recommend this company to friends or tell them about someone else? Should I buy from this company again or look for a new vendor? Does it make sense to like this business on Facebook, or will the business just fill my feed with useless crap? Why would consumers roll the dice when they can roll the tape and assess the histories of their relationships with brands?

If their ledgers are too new or if a brand just appeared on their radar, consumers will turn to external evidence to fill the ledger. Instead of "This is how they treat me," it becomes "This is how they treat a consumer *like* me, according to angry posts on their Facebook page," or "This is how they treat the environment, according to a blog I read and trust." If that ledger gets filled with enough negative third-party content, consumers won't try the brand. This is the magic of sites like Yelp—how much spending and frustration have you avoided simply by checking Yelp reviews before you try new restaurants? In my case, it's hard to imagine traveling without it!

Facebook is beginning to make decisions for consumers by watching how they interact with brands and using the data to adjust how often consumers are exposed to those brands through the Facebook platform. If a company's posts are receiving a lot of negative signals—being flagged for spam or hidden at a higher than usual rate—Facebook will interpret this as a signal that the posts are low quality and won't serve them up to as many users going forward.[23]

The path to success for brands in the Social-Industrial Revolution is not one of deception, paid audiences, silenced critics, or competitive chicanery. Technology, in this case, is an epic simplifying force. Companies that focus on providing better experiences will be rewarded by hyperconnected consumers. Companies that cling to the old ways will be punished by the same consumers that reward the agility and openness of their competitors. In a sense, this is a truer version of the free market, a purer expression of the economic principles that the West, and more recently, the world, has embraced. The best now wins on its own merit, in a competition that anyone can watch. Entry is free or inexpensive, and the large and comfortable are increasingly threatened by the small and ambitious. New relationships and exchanges of value are forming between consumers and companies, creating a universe of opportunity for participants in all walks of life. As siloes of data and the walls between people crumble, fascinating new models emerge, innovation accelerates, and average people discover powers that they never knew they possessed. We don't need to sit back and wait to see if this optimistic view is realized, because this revolution is happening at the speed of social media. We're simultaneously witnesses and participants, journalists and historians, uniquely situated and single actors in something much larger.

CHEAT SHEET

- Want to get an unresponsive company's attention? Take your complaint public by posting to the company's Facebook wall, blog, product reviews, and wherever else your complaint will be subject to public scrutiny.
- Brands may be losing influence, but they can identify influential consumers and work with them to reach new audiences. Influence is currency, and expectations of compensation are rising.
- The only way to advance in this economy is to deliver exactly what the consumer wants. No need to guess; the data is out there.

CHAPTER 8

The Birth of Big Social

Woe to those who underestimate the power of Big Social.

I've seen the expression "wake the beast" used a lot in reference to social media, but the expression never fit—you can't "wake" something that *never sleeps*, or, more accurately, has *never slept*.

Social media has been big, powerful, and constantly active for a long time. It's a largely passive landscape, in which a tiny minority of users actively participate, while the vast majority of users "lurk" (the 1 percent rule I wrote about earlier). But the concentrations of activity can spring up organically, as when something goes viral; or they can be predictable, like the spike in Twitter use on Election Day in the United States and during the World Cup.

It's much more difficult to manufacture such activity levels, and it's harder still to concentrate that activity and direct it into real progress against a shared goal. In their short history, social media "victories" have been more accident than alignment, more carpet bomb than precision strike.

One of these corporate apologies is not like the others:

At Gap brand, our customers have always come first. We've been listening to and watching all of the comments this past week. We heard them say over and over again they are passionate about our blue box logo, and they want it back. So we've made the decision to do just that—we will bring it back across all channels.

It is clear from the feedback over the past two months that many members felt we lacked respect and humility in the way we announced the separation of DVD and streaming and the price changes. That was certainly not our intent, and I offer my sincere apology. Let me explain what we are doing.

We have observed a spike in domain name transfers, which are running above normal rates and which we attribute to GoDaddy's prior support for SOPA.

The first two apologies (Gap and Netflix, respectively) respond to the *raw* power of social media. Dissent gone viral, reaching a fever pitch. A familiar kind of outcry.

The third (GoDaddy) responds to something new. I call it Big Social.

New Expectations

Big Social is self-aware. It knows the extent of its access. It understands the influence it wields. It has learned how to carry itself with confidence and how to direct fire with pinpoint precision. And it has a new set of expectations.

The expectations of the power holders are being realigned, as well. The short history of WeThePeople.org, an online petition platform created by the White House as "a new way to petition the Obama Administration to take action," is a lesson in real-time expectation setting. When the site launched in 2011, petitions that received 5,000 online signatures within 30 days were guaranteed an official White House response. That threshold was later adjusted to

25,000 and again to 100,000. According to an explanatory post on the White House blog (yes, that exists) by the director of digital strategy, Macon Phillips, "None of us knew how popular it would be, but it's exceeded our wildest expectations."[1] The math is extraordinary:

> In the first 10 months of 2012, it took an average of 18 days for a new petition to cross the 25,000-signature threshold. In the last two months of the year, that average time was cut in half to just 9 days, and most petitions that crossed the threshold collected 25,000 signatures within five days of their creation. More than 60 percent of the petitions to cross the threshold in all of 2012 did so in the last two months of the year.

The administration, the administration argues, isn't able to offer official responses to so many petitions. The unofficial storyline is more interesting. As soon as Obama was reelected, the site was hit with a reactionary wave of petitions from all 50 states that sought secession, which together have received over 900,000 signatures.[2] In some states, such as North Dakota and Hawaii, the number of petition signatures was equivalent to more than 1 percent of state residents.[3] Many of the petitions crossed the then-threshold of 25,000 signatures, and the fact that the White House was being forced (by its own rules) to respond to these extreme proposals had to have spooked the White House workers.

Impossible to Ignore

Political institutions, generally the enemies of access, are no longer able to ignore the role of social media in providing access to power and information. "I think we've seen really interesting early days here, but if we're talking about networked democracy, you have to remember that it's just in its infancy," says Alex Howard, Washington correspondent with *O'Reilly Radar*. In an e-mail to me, Howard noted:

Policy makers, particularly government officials and staffers, are overwhelmed by the incoming flood of messages as it is. That's something that became quite apparent when email entered the picture in the nineties, and then the growth of other kinds of communications since then has only accelerated that. As some people have pointed out, notably Clay Johnson, what Congress actually needs is to grow bigger ears to be able to listen to all of that, and to know who in that huge amount of incoming requests, ideas, feedback, etc., are their constituents—the people that they are supposed to represent.

When Big Social Came to Town

The defeat of SOPA (Stop Online Privacy Act) will be remembered as the perfect demonstration of all the ways social media has changed access to institutional power and influence on corporate policy. But more specifically, it may be remembered as the birth of Big Social. The bill sought "to expand the ability of U.S. law enforcement to fight online trafficking in copyrighted intellectual property and counterfeit goods" through blocking access to supposedly offending websites and other means.[4] It had the support of massive lobbying groups like the Motion Picture Association of America and the Recording Industry Association of America, corporations like Time Warner and Pfizer, and majority support in both the House and Senate.

Opponents felt that SOPA would cause irreparable harm to the structure of the Internet, lead to censorship, stifle innovation, and prevent those harmed from appealing. The legislation had large and visible corporate opponents, including Google, Twitter, Wikipedia, and Yahoo, so it was by no means an entirely grassroots effort. SOPA had been a popular topic on countless blogs and across social media channels for months before the legislation was to be voted on. During that time, traditional media ignored the story. From late October 2011 to mid-January 2012, the major networks ran 41 stories about Tim Tebow, 14 about Casey Anthony, 9 on Kim Kardashian's divorce, and just 2 on SOPA, according to Media Matters, which observed that "the parent companies of these networks, as well as two of the networks themselves," were official SOPA supporters.[5] SOPA opponents used social media to spread a boycott of companies that supported the legislation, most notably GoDaddy; and after losing 37,000 domains in just two days, GoDaddy officially reversed its position.[6]

Closing in on the scheduled vote, 23 percent of adults aged 18 to 29 followed news about the SOPA legislation more closely than any other topic.[7] The story would not be contained and was entering the mainstream dialogue *in spite of* the mainstream media. On January 18, 2012, social media activists and SOPA's corporate opponents orchestrated a national day of protest in combination with a "blackout" of many of the world's most popular sites. The protest took SOPA from the technical and theoretical to the tangible by illustrating what SOPA would mean to everyday citizens and giving them simple ways to contribute to the fight. Nearly 2.5 million SOPA-related posts flooded Twitter, a million people sent e-mails to their representatives, and millions more signed online petitions—all in a single day.[8] Lawmakers suddenly had overwhelming evidence that if they voted for SOPA, they would risk losing political capital and, possibly, their next race. Key SOPA supporters began to distance themselves from the bill and then, realizing that equivocation wouldn't be tolerated, switched sides. The bill was shelved indefinitely. American politicians and tone-deaf corporations had reckoned with a new power dynamic. Like a guerilla force, it can be quickly mobilized and attack with full fury just as easily as it can recede into the landscape and allow normality to return, until the next battle. Like the best sort of muckraking journalism, it exhibits a collective sense of duty—and no uncertain amount of glee in—exposing hidden power structures and shaming perceived transgressors into obedience.

SOPA was the first battle with Big Social, and Big Social won.

Can Big Social Be Bought?

Activists have taken well to social media because it maps perfectly to the grassroots framework that has been their only true means of success outside of litigation. Big Social has the potential to make up with action what activists lack in funds. They can't go toe-to-toe with opponents on the airwaves with ads, they don't have the purchased political clout of large donors, and they're excluded from the old-boy networks of Washington and state capitals. So they take to the streets and, now, to the social web to get the word out and mobilize their base. And they're doing this so well that they're forcing opponents to step it up. Lobbyists, who tend to do their jobs behind closed doors and through traditional media outreach, are adapting to the scrappy new-era tactics of their activist opponents.

This dynamic is playing out in the story of Keystone XL, an environmental hot-button issue since 2008. Keystone XL is a proposed extension of the existing Keystone pipeline that runs from Alberta, Canada, through Nebraska and several other states, to refineries in Illinois and Oklahoma. The extension would bring oil-rich tar sands all the way to the Gulf Coast of Texas, and according to environmentalist groups and a number of politicians, it would negatively impact several environmentally sensitive areas along the way. The activists have suffered a string of familiar, frustrating defeats, ranging from government approvals of continued pipeline construction to losses in court. But President Obama's second inaugural address, which expressed a "renewed commitment to environmental concerns," has given the activists the dose of strength to rally on the social web.[9] Among their successes, a slate of popular YouTube videos, a bustling Facebook page, and antipipeline posts from a ring of "high-profile bloggers." In the face of the vibrant, effective social presence of their opponents, the threat of a battle with Big Social looms.

But what if Big Social could be made to fight *for* Big Energy instead of against it? The energy industry and surrounding groups, normally reliant on traditional political maneuvering, have ventured into the unfamiliar but crucial territory with a social media campaign of their own. It spans all the battlefronts the environmentalists are dominating—Facebook, YouTube, Twitter, etc.—and is generating respectable activity levels. Whether it is effective is yet to be determined, but what the effort represents is more important for our purposes. What we're seeing is perhaps the most traditional industry in America—oil and gas—realizing that without investing in social media to access powerful constituencies, it may actually lose this fight.

Most of the stories in this book concern access to the elite, but this tale of Keystone XL is quite the opposite; here we have an industry that has *never* had a problem accessing decision makers (all the way up to heads of state), but it has found itself without unfettered access to everyday people. Everyday people DVR-hop over commercials and live much of their lives connected to social networks, where ads are easy to ignore. Opinions in the social web are shaped by "people like me," "people I know," and "people I want to know." Unless these three groups are supporting the oil and gas industry through their words and actions, it doesn't stand a chance with everyday people. This is the first phase of a calculated social media presence for the establishment.

And this is just the beginning of Big Social. We don't know what its next target is or how big it will get. But it's safe to say there's no going back.

CHAPTER 9

Media Ladders and the Art of the Newsjack

This may sound like heresy, but I'm a big fan of traditional media. I'm absolutely critical of it, but I'm not dismissive of its raw power and reach. Social media side doors are a kind of "hack," and traditional media is still a universe of gatekeepers, barriers to entry, and huge audiences. In other words, to access traditional media platforms via the side door is the *ultimate hack*.

Media Laddering

It's a mistake to pour *all* your energy into scraping together your own platform, blog post by blog post, tweet by tweet, connection by connection. Save some of those cycles for finding a way onto someone else's platform. I call this media laddering. Media laddering, in practice, is using your social media presence and skills to find your way onto a larger platform. When it comes to national audiences, TV, radio, magazines, and newspapers have done the heavy lifting for decades—sometimes centuries—to build them. That reach isn't going away anytime soon, and while we new media types love to talk about shrinking ad revenues and postcaptive audiences, few of us can really hold a candle to the reach of an institution like CNN or the *Economist*. We love to knock them and hate that we need them. But we'd be naive—and in a way, irresponsible—to write them off. And in advertising, big money still buys big audiences. I celebrated Oreo's brilliantly adaptive tweet during the 2013 Super Bowl blackout ("Power out? No problem. You can still dunk in the dark.") like everyone else, but it reached a potential audience of 13.3 million, while TV ads reached a potential audience of 110 million viewers.[1]

Media outreach is complicated and difficult. Victories come in bursts of coverage, which are typically few and far between. News gets stale fast in the 24/7 media environment, and most organizations aren't nimble enough to be consistently relevant and newsworthy. Press releases are less and less effective (but relationships still matter, as we've discussed extensively in this book). Individuals, however, have the agility to keep up—yet they usually lack resources and depth of experience.

Right now, social ads are cheap, targeted, and easy to optimize in real time. They aren't yet particularly effective for selling products directly, as many advertisers are lamenting. As my social job search proved, side doors can open when people take something familiar—like social ads—and apply an unfamiliar twist. Social ads can be used to get noticed by media professionals and ladder up to their vast platforms.

The Guest Pitch

This technique involves marketing yourself as an on-air expert guest or source for print. Create individualized ads for each network or outlet you'd like to pursue. For example, for CNN, the headline might read "Hi, CNN" or "CNN employee?" In other words, something that contrasts starkly with the one-size-fits-all headlines most people just ignore. Choose an image of your face—research shows human faces are highly emotionally engaging, which is one theory of why Facebook itself is so popular.[2] The ad copy will need to accomplish three things with ruthless brevity. First, establish your expertise. Second, tell your target why it should care or how it will benefit. Third, make the next step clear with a call to action. Altogether, it might read something like this ad.

> **Hi, CNN. I'm Ian.**
> daretocomment.com
>
> I'm the perfect expert for your next social media story. Click to learn more.

The ad is just one step in the journey. Link it to something that shows why you would make a good guest and make it *absurdly* easy to contact you. In my case, I created a custom page on my blog that welcomes media professionals, lists my credentials and some of the coverage I've earned, and provides three means of contact. I stripped out a lot of the potentially distracting elements of my site that could compete with my primary goal: contact. The results of my own tests were mixed. The ads got me access but not influence. Clicks but no contact. On Facebook, I got 27 clicks from employees of the *New York Times,* BBC, and WNYC, $18.65 spent. The average click-through rate (CTR) of 0.10 percent was low, but the clicks were cheap, at about $0.69 each. On LinkedIn, I was able to target more outlets at a higher total CTR of 0.23 percent: 70 clicks from employees of BBC, CNN, the *Wall Street Journal,* Fox News, Associated Press, and NBC. In all, $140.62 spent, which amounts to $2.01 per click. LinkedIn summarizes clicks by seniority, industry, and job function. The BBC ad, which received the most clicks, garnered the clicks primarily from senior broadcast media professionals in the media and communication function, which seems to me like a fairly qualified audience.

The Content Pitch

This technique focuses on content. Targeting people with existing audiences to carry forward your message is the backbone of PR. Yet using social ads for this purpose is virtually unheard of in the PR industry. I did find one exception. PR and marketing agency aimClear has used Facebook and LinkedIn ads to promote "compelling content designed for the media, [who] become interested in the promoted content, and follow the story on their own volition."[3]

The key here is to align subject matter to audience. Your ideal audience members are interested in your subject matter *and* occupy content-creation or media roles themselves. Imagine, for example, you've been hired by the Romanian government to boost American tourism to Transylvania, and you're planning distribution of a "Transylvanian getaway" YouTube series. Even if the content is incredible, promoting it directly to the end consumers will only give you access to their average-size social networks; your reach will be limited.

Rather, your priority should be targeting people with access to huge audiences—media professionals. Like end consumers, they use LinkedIn and Facebook, where they've self-identified their interests, roles, employers, hometowns, group memberships, and more. LinkedIn will let you zero in on employees of National Geographic, Where Publishing, Discovery Channel, Travel Channel, and countless other travel media companies. You can also target by groups like World Wide Travel Writers, Travel Media Pros, and Travel Editors & Freelance Journalists.

Think of targeting like a Venn diagram. You can go wide and target based on one revealing criterion, like industry group membership. But you may end up paying more in total, and your audience will be less qualified than if you take the narrow, or "long tail," approach, which involves two or more qualifying criteria. For example, you could target people that self-identify (1) as writers and (2) as members of the Travel Media Pros group. This overlap of qualifiers means the people who see your ad are likely travel writers.

With this technique, you don't want to make your pitch too transparent in the ad. It should be compelling because the headline, the copy, and the content it references are compelling—not because it reveals your marketing savvy and targeting wherewithal. LinkedIn also has a new 30-second video ad format that seems promising, and it would be ideal for this imaginary project or even a "hire-me" campaign.

It's important to understand that the effectiveness of this technique doesn't stem from its unique and surprising nature. Its power lies, in a sense, in its gentleness. It's not pushy, like the usual pitches reporters receive. This approach lives or dies by the quality of the ad—from headline to copy to photo—and, ultimately, by the story it tells. As Lindsay Schleisman of aimClear writes, "Social ads are not a disruptive form of pitching . . . the reporter clicks on the ad, indicating interest in the concept," which is both a way to qualify the target and a way to hone one's storytelling and copywriting skills.

Unless you live in a top 10 market, you'll need a way to reach the first rung of the media ladder, since your local affiliate stations and papers likely will not have enough listed employees on Facebook or LinkedIn to be a targetable group. You can still reach them if you can locate the Facebook profiles of their decision makers and on-air talent. I may not be able to select the employees of KVUE (Austin's ABC News affiliate) as an audience, but I can find their producers, talent, and other employees on Facebook and create my own audience.

Climbing Up

It's a mistake to think of any media outlet as truly independent. Like the rungs of a ladder, every media outlet, whether "new" or "traditional," is connected to outlets beneath it. The bottom rungs have smaller audiences and, usually, lower standards governing the stories they cover and the sources they turn to. Moving up the ladder, audiences and ad revenues get bigger, and coverage decisions are more discriminating, but source material is often mined from the outlets one or two rungs down. This ladder goes all the way to the top of the media landscape.

It's a symbiotic relationship between media rungs; the bigger guys get the material they need to keep up with demand and impression goals, and the smaller guys get precious links and referral traffic. Unless the rules are broken (like failing to attribute material or poaching exclusive sources), the rungs get along.

In his book *Trust Me, I'm Lying: Confessions of a Media Manipulator*, Ryan Holiday calls the way stories move from smaller to larger markets "trading up the chain." Holiday's exploits tend to incorporate a fair amount of deception and trickery, but the media structure he describes can be conquered without sacrificing one's integrity (though it may take longer). He points readers to a post from middle-tier blogger Lindsay Robertson, who makes many of the exact same claims as Holiday, but from the other side of the equation. Robertson describes the strategy of someone she calls "Brilliant Online Publicist":

> *While the rest of the publicists in her company were sending out mass emails to everyone, hoping to get bites from* Perez Hilton, Gawker, HuffPo, *or wherever, this publicist focused on a lower traffic tier with the (correct) understanding that these days, content filters up as much as it filters down, and often the smaller sites, with their ability to dig deeper into the internet and be more nimble, act as farm teams for the larger ones. A site can be*

enormously influential without having crazy eyeballs, because all eyeballs are not equal. MANY times—I would say almost every time—that I posted one of her client's items on my site, they were linked back within hours by the big guys, who probably would have tuned her out otherwise.[4]

Finding the Starting Rung

A slew of "freemium" tools can help you determine which blogs are feeding content to higher-tier outlets. One of them is called Open Site Explorer, from SEOmoz. I used it to take a look at my friend Jason Falls's popular blog *Social Media Explorer*. Plugging the URL into the search box, I found links from CNN, *Forbes, Entrepreneur, Inc, Huffington Post, Fast Company, Business Insider,* and many more outlets I'd love to appear on. Naturally, I'll consider pitching my next guest post to *SME*. Other tools with similar functionality include Majestic SEO and Ahrefs Site Explorer.

Access Is the Easy Part

How do you find journalists and bloggers who have demonstrated interest in the thing you want to talk about? And what's your next move? Greg Galant, the CEO of Sawhorse Media, created a platform called Muck Rack to help answer these questions (see the Quick Reference section at the back of the book for more about it). Journalists aren't always posting about current and upcoming story subjects, and it's rarer still to see them make public requests for sources over social media (although this does happen occasionally). "There's a lot more value in digging the well before you're thirsty," Galant observes. He stresses the importance of building relationships, whenever possible, *before* you have something to pitch. "Sometimes, there's a story they're working on that you should be in, and if you're top of mind, you may find yourself in it." Social media helps people reach out to journalists by being useful to them, helping them chase down a lead, facilitating an introduction, or giving them the perfect quote. "Journalists need ideas, and although they get hundreds of emails a day, most of them aren't helpful," Galant tells me. "You can do your research using social media to find out what they're working on, or what they really are interested in."

My conversation with Galant made me realize that, with journalists, sending them a message—getting access—is the easy part. They all need tips; even at top outlets, many reporters publish their e-mail addresses and phone numbers. What social media does is lend *gravity* to that access. It makes your message, however you send it, stand out. It might stand out because you've done your homework, and you really have a sense of what a journalist is going to write about next. Or it might stand out because the recipients can associate the "from" line on your e-mail with a helpful interaction they had on Twitter, so they don't ignore it.

Newsjacking

If you're reading this book, you're probably not a media darling, recurring guest, or paid pundit. You don't have access to audiences like they do. Think about the people you read about, watch on TV, or hear on the radio. In terms of how they got there, they usually fall into one of four categories.

1. **Creators.** This doesn't necessarily mean they faked the story; it means these people did something with the intention of getting media coverage, or they tried to get media coverage for something not previously considered newsworthy.
2. **Participants.** These people are participants in a story that gets picked up. Whatever they did wasn't designed for the media, and in many cases, they would rather not be participants in the

first place. The media pursues them as part of the story, and not the other way around. Often they just happen to fit within a story's narrative, and they're in the right place at the right time.

3. **Known quantities.** They may have been news creators or partic-ipants in the past, but now they are in the media because they are familiar to producers and audiences; their appearances are predictable and quotable. Former Clinton political advisor Dick Morris fits this profile like a glove.

4. **Anglers.** These people sidle up to stories, explore new angles, and place unique spins on unfolding news: a blogger humor-ously skewering the Kardashian clan or a professor releasing unique findings about cyberbullying. They are anglers to existing stories, and the media likes them because the core stories have already been road-tested with an audience, so to add something new to them lends just enough freshness to continue the coverage for another cycle, until the reporters find the next angler—or until people lose interest.

Bold and contrarian voices make great anglers. I remember an angler-rich narrative very vividly, the idea that "national debt doesn't matter." It became a story itself because it was such a rad-ical departure from the mainstream media conversation. It just had to be explored, if only to be ridiculed as out of touch, wrong-headed, and subject to just about every other pejorative phrase you can imagine. I didn't really care, at the time, whether it was true or not. I was interested in the way the counternarrative received mainstream attention, and I learned that it did so *because* it was a counternarrative—it was another way to rekindle interest in the same story. Soon, I saw that formula everywhere I looked, and I still do. Pundits, for instance, are not paid to be correct—they are featured, essentially, for the boldness of their predictions and for their stage presence while making them. In fact, one noted study shows that political pundits' predictions "have a rate of success that is only slightly greater than that of random chance."[5]

I'm discussing these categories not to belittle one or to glorify another. I'm interested in strategic effectiveness, and it's through that lens that I wonder why so many media hopefuls pursue creator strategies. A stunt will usually be seen and covered as such. Trying to make something that has little external appeal into a wider story requires a special touch, an abundance of luck—and, usually, an exaggerated sense of self-importance.

The smart money is on the anglers. They are the ones who recognize and accept the humbling truth that we don't choose what the media portrays, unless we are the media. Your best chance of accessing audiences is to tell them something new about something they care about.

Newsjacking is the modern angler's weapon of choice. According to David Meerman Scott, who coined the term *newsjacking* and wrote a book of the same name, newsjacking is "the process by which you inject your ideas or angles into breaking news, in real-time, in order to generate media coverage for yourself or your business." I asked him about the element of speed. He responded:

> *What's changed recently is that Google now indexes in real-time. That allows a timely blog post to be seen by journalists as they search for more information on a topic. Real-time is the key here. Yet nearly all PR people are in campaign mode rather than real-time mode, so those like us who understand newsjacking have an advantage.*

Google is constantly tweaking its core algorithm to reflect evolving user preferences and expectations. Google users, increasingly, value content freshness as a key ingredient in a rewarding experience, and so Google has released several updates that, in many contexts, favor newer content over older content. This includes content that isn't wholly new, but partially updated or refreshed, and signals of continued relevance to users, like comment activity. These adjustments are an equalizer and can give the quick a very real edge over the slow moving.

You can piggyback on breaking news by piggybacking on larger platforms, too. While quickly getting up a blog post is ideal, your blog may not be able to handle the influx of traffic if your newsjacking tactics are successful, or you may not feel your blog is ready for prime time. Not to worry, there are other ways to get your message up quickly without using your own platform. You can record and upload a video to YouTube, put a slide deck or PDF together and host it on SlideShare, or publicly share a longer-format social post (Google+ and Facebook work well for this). Tumblr is great for newsjacking, too, as you can set up a story-specific account in a matter of minutes.

A single post is easily buried in the avalanche of content surrounding a breaking story. To really grab attention, you need to post frequently, address developments as they hit the headlines, get more and more fresh content indexed by search engines, and appear at the top of social feeds. The more you post, the more you'll be noticed. It can be effective to break a larger post into sections and then post each individually throughout the day. Developing stories normally have a reigning hashtag or a few in competition for the crown. If your tweets have room to spare, it's wise to add the most popular hashtags for the topic. Twitter is more of a meritocracy than other networks, and interesting, timely, and relevant content can go viral without any consideration of its originator's perceived influence.

WTHashtag.com tracks and ranks trending hashtags and allows users to place them in context by adding definitions. My favorite tool for joining and monitoring hashtag-based conversations is TweetChat.com, which allows you to pause, slow down the flow of content, highlight specific users, and share content directly to the conversation without manually appending the hashtag every time. TrendsMap.com visualizes popular hashtags by location (city, country) to detect regional trends, and it also identifies globally trending users.

Link to external posts and mention other experts as you build out your content to take advantage of pingbacks, vanity alerts, and vanity searches. Remember, people like to share things that mention them, and if they share your posts, you reach their audience.

In an environment so full of self-promotion and one-to-many trumpeting, the easiest way to cut through the noise is to be curious, conversational, and helpful. Ask questions of topic influencers, tell them what you think of the points they make, or add your own perspective to theirs. To be helpful, you can do things like create lists of topic experts and central figures, look out for questions surrounding a story they are writing about, and then do your best to be the one who answers those questions first or best. You can actually use Twitter's search function (twitter.com/search-advanced) to show only questions related to specific hashtags by typing your query without the # symbol into the field "These hashtags" and checking the "Question?" box at the bottom.

While monitoring a developing story, people are usually confronted with too little signal (information they want) and too much noise (a combination of information they don't want, repetition, and anything else that exceeds their processing capacity). Thus, to become indispensable, create a destination. Google hangouts are perfect for creating temporary destinations to share information and discuss breaking news, and they can be promoted easily. During Hurricane Sandy, Accuweather set up a Google hangout with three meteorologists to answer viewer questions in real time. I love that example because it demonstrates so vividly the fact that newsjacking and exploitation are far from the same thing.[6] Live blogging and curation can be used to great effect by providing a single, story-specific home for updates and resources through a human filter (you). I've seen it done well with Storify and ScribbleLive.

Snapping up the right web domain as a story breaks can take your newsjacking to a whole new level. According to CNN.com, it only took 90 seconds from the moment Mitt Romney uttered the bizarre phrase "binders full of women" to the registration of bindersfullof-women.com. Chris Harris, who worked for the super PAC that bought the domain, was waiting for the right newsjacking opportunity: "We were sort of on standby, knowing that Internet memes like this can solidify within seconds." Rather than build a site just to exploit the humorous meme, the American Bridge 21st Century PAC whipped up a dedicated Tumblr post and had it humming the next morning. Concurrently, a Binders Full of Women Facebook page "drew more than 250,000 'likes' in less than 12 hours."[7] Two parody Twitter accounts together racked up 20,000 overnight.

Our expectation of immediacy is reaching a point where brands are actually being criticized for not newsjacking fast enough. In another widely parodied political moment (politics is fertile ground for newsjackers), Marco Rubio awkwardly reached for a bottle of Poland Spring water while delivering the Republican State of the Union response, and the moment instantly went viral. Poland Spring didn't ride the unexpected wave of interest in its brand until the following day, when it posted a photo of a Poland Spring bottle in front of a dressing room makeup mirror with the caption, "Reflecting on our cameo. What a night!" Late to the game as it was (by current standards), the post had received over 6,000 likes, 815 shares, and 239 comments in the 11 days after the visual gaffe occurred. Yet when compared with Marco Rubio's response that night (tweeting a photo of the famous bottle), which earned him 13,000 new followers overnight and generated enough coverage to help offset the awkwardness of the sip, it's clear that Poland Springs could have acted much more quickly to capitalize on its moment in the spotlight. As Ryu Spaeth of the *Week* observed, "One quick-thinking tweet could have capitalized on the slurp heard around the world."[8] Yet @PolandSpringWtr and two other possible official accounts have each been dormant for a year or more. @PolandSpringWtr appears to have been made private after the "incident," probably out of embarrassment for the brand's uninspired social media presence. As with Romney's binders gaffe, meme-related domains were snapped up that evening, including thirstyrubio.com, rubiowaterbottle.com, rubiowater.com, rubioswig.com, rubioswaterbottle.com, rubioswater.com, and several more (this continued into the next several days).[9]

Consider using social ads in your newsjacking attempt. As always, keep your ear to the ground and be ready to move at a moment's notice. Sometimes you'll know a story is coming up, like a scheduled press conference or political debate, and you can get the wheels in motion beforehand by outlining your content in advance, preparing the landing page, and anticipating what will be deemed newsworthy. Consider the debate example: you know only one side can win, so you may prepare skeleton content and ads for both eventualities (e.g., "Why [Candidate A] Won," "Why [Candidate B] Lost," "Why [Candidate B] Won," "Why [Candidate A] Lost." This is an old news industry trick, preparing graphics, headlines, and even obituaries in advance.

You should also have your targeting schema planned in advance, which isn't difficult since you know the kinds of stories that specific types of journalists work on. For the debate example above, your list might include anyone with the job title of political reporter or political editor, or you might select the names of people with more general titles like correspondent or journalist as long as their residence is given as *Washington, D.C.*

When the story breaks, whether you anticipated it or not, you need to get your content and ad up as quickly as possible. This isn't a time for perfectionism—if you're familiar with the term *minimally viable product,* this is when your job is to create it—something that's good enough to get the viewer to the next step. If the story in your area of expertise is truly unanticipated and you haven't prepared anything, your first step is still getting the ads up, since they can take up to 24 hours to approve. As you're waiting for approval, craft your unique point of view and create your landing page.

CHEAT SHEET

- Social ads can be targeted at employees at news organizations. A number of strategies can make these ads enticing to the media:
  - Pitching oneself as a subject-matter expert
  - Showcasing interesting content to specific audiences
  - Sharing a unique point of view or insight about a hot story (newsjacking)
- Create Twitter lists of the journalists covering your beat, interact with them, and watch for opportunities to help them with stories.
- Journalists tend to be *technically* accessible, but their in-boxes are so saturated with bad pitches, reaching them via social media can cut through the noise and earn their attention.
- Your best chance of accessing audiences is to tell them something new about something they care about (the angler strategy).
- The keys to successful newsjacking campaigns are:
  - Having something fresh to say about a breaking story
  - Creating content quickly and updating it as the story progresses
  - Making your content discoverable (e.g., using relevant hashtags)
  - Linking your content to the work of others
  - Seeking questions and providing answers

CHAPTER 10

Secrets of
Social Advertising

"Why haven't I been e-mailed or called yet?" I asked myself this question a few times a day, refreshing my in-box more often than I'm proud of. I was obsessed. My ad was getting more clicks than I expected, driving visitors to the landing page on my blog I had made just for them and had hidden from Google so as not to pollute the data. I could draw the kind of direct pathways web geeks dream of. The 18 clicks LinkedIn reported on Tuesday matched the 18 visits WordPress had logged for the landing page, which was driving a few clicks a day back to my LinkedIn profile. I could even determine, more often than not, the exact profile someone was looking at when they clicked on my ad (all the visitors were strangers). I had all the data I needed to know something wasn't working. But what was it?

Unlike some of the other tests I've done while researching this book, this LinkedIn experiment had a strong ulterior motive. In October 2012, LinkedIn unveiled its Influencer program, allowing users to follow "the most influential thought leaders on LinkedIn" as they shared "unique knowledge and professional insights."[1] The marquee thought leaders were people like Richard Branson and Barack Obama, but I was intrigued to learn that some of the people LinkedIn selected weren't exactly household names.

About a week after Influencer was introduced, I learned that LinkedIn was accepting applications for the program, so I sent mine in. I never heard back, contrary to the application's claim that users would find out within a week. I wasn't upset, as I suspected LinkedIn simply got overwhelmed with interest. Months later, when I was brainstorming ways to test LinkedIn's ads, I thought of the Influencer program again. The goal crystalized: use ads to become an Influencer.

The ads I ran were all variations on this (which is also the first ad that appears in the figure):

[Headline] *I'm influencer material*
[Body] *Consider me for your Influencer content program. Click for more info!*

I targeted 3,784 LinkedIn employees in North America, and I bid up to $2.37 per click. After three days, I had 31 clicks: 71 percent senior level, 25.8 percent manager level, and 3.2 percent director level. But none of them led to any inbound activity after hitting my landing page, which was a pitch for an Influencer program spot. My call to action urged visitors to contact me by phone, e-mail, LinkedIn, or Twitter. I expected *someone* would reach out or at least send my information to a colleague more qualified to talk about the Influencer program.

I had a hunch that the call to action, and not the ad, was the problem. People weren't reaching out directly because they didn't want to talk to a stranger about a program they had nothing to do with. Maybe my ad was being sent around LinkedIn in the course of those three days, but it clearly wasn't reaching the right people. I needed to tell visitors *exactly* which colleague to contact on my behalf, instead of asking them to waste time talking to me or pulling up an organizational chart to find the Influencer program's owner.

I'm Influencer material
Consider me for your Influencer content
program. Click for more info!

From: McGraw-Hill

Go To URL: http://daretocomment.com/hi-linkedin/

Let's make it official.
I'd love to contribute content as an official
Influencer. Click for info.

From: McGraw-Hill

Go To URL: http://daretocomment.com/hi-linkedin/

This ad = proof.
I know social. Select me for your Influencer
program! Click to learn more.

From: McGraw-Hill

Go To URL: http://daretocomment.com/hi-linkedin/

I found a few blog posts that identified the person in charge of the program: Daniel Roth, LinkedIn's executive editor. That evening, I rewrote the call to action on the landing page to trigger the ricochet effect I was after: "You can help by asking Daniel Roth [link to his profile], LinkedIn's Executive Editor, to give me a chance!" I didn't have Daniel's e-mail address, but LinkedIn obviously did!

The following evening, Roth e-mailed me:

*Hey, excellent use of LinkedIn ads :). You available to chat
tomorrow?*

We spoke by phone, and he told me that my strategy had become "quite the sensation" at LinkedIn. The Influencer program would be opening up to new members in a few months, and could I give him a call then?

In hindsight, it's simple. You don't need to reach someone directly if you make it easy for the people around that person to reach out on your behalf. Don't expect your audience to make the choice you would make if given the same set of options, and realize that people are more willing to help if what you're asking for is well within their comfort zone. I started out by asking people to contact a total stranger (me). Nothing. Later, I asked people to contact a colleague. Less than a day later, their colleague contacted *me*.

Revisiting the Social Job Ad

I wouldn't be writing this book if I hadn't discovered the job-hunting power of Facebook ads back in early 2010. Maybe a different book, but not this one. So I decided to revisit the technique three years later to see if, after the "secret" was out, the method still worked. I ran two ads targeted at 16,560 users "who live in the United States, age 25 or older, who graduated from college, who work at Google." I used a head shot for the picture and tried to make the copy snappy, just like last time. I came up with two versions.

The custom landing page I created on my blog spilled the beans:

Thanks for clicking, but I have to come clean with you. I'm not actually looking for a job. This is a test to see how effective social ads are for job-hunting. I'm writing a book about stuff like this.

The campaign reached 6,947 Googlers and received 48 clicks (0.103 percent CTR), all at a total cost of $30.68. Forget about metrics for a second, and ask yourself, "If I was looking for a job at

Future Googler.
daretocomment.com

That's me, with your help. Click to learn why I'd make a great colleague.

I googled "future boss"
daretocomment.com

Your name came up. Also, pictures of robots. Click to learn why I'd be great at Google.

Google and I could somehow pay $30.68 for 48 Google employees to see a web page I created just for them, would it be worth it?" If you answered no, I'd really like to hear your strategy!

One Googler was skeptical that this type of ad would sustainably yield results:

> *The really random ad text about robots was bizarre and eye catching. I do wonder, however, if job seekers all adopted the same strategy of bizarre headline and ad text in social media contexts, saturation might weaken this strategy and make it a much lower ROI marketing effort for job seekers.*

I agree that saturation would indeed weaken the effect of these ads. But I thought that about the ads I placed in March 2010, and the saturation has not occurred. If and when it does, we'll find better tactics. But I don't see it happening any time soon. Remember, most people are comfortable with standing in line. They like routines. They like known quantities. This strategy could go completely viral, and I still doubt that the effect would be dulled significantly—think about all the open jobs, hiring managers, and candidates out there who will never do anything like this. The kind of people who would take out social job ads are also the kind of people who would quickly find creative alternatives should the ads become ineffective.

This was a blanket ad, but targeting could have been improved in a number of ways. I could have limited the ad to Googlers who live in California (where Google has its headquarters) or to people who mentioned an interest in marketing or social media. At a company as large as Google, I think it's wise to produce a few separate ads to target different subsets of employees. For example, I could try reaching out to Google HR with a unique spin:

[Headline] *Google HR?*
[Body] *Human: Check. Resources: I have them. Ipso facto, I'd be great at Google. Click for info!*

While the audience of Google employees with HR-related interests on Facebook is approximately 100 people, as long as the ad stands out and earns clicks in the direction of my credentials and work history, it can be extremely successful.

The Ultimate Social Ad Side Door, Hidden in Plain Sight

In the space of a few days, Mark Zuckerberg has seen my ad 7 times. Marissa Meyer, Yahoo's CEO, has seen another ad of mine 39 times. This has cost me *nothing*. Zero dollars, zero cents.

The first click was exhilarating. It came from Facebook and hit the campaign-specific landing page I had created on my blog. The moment I saw the visitor on my real-time analytics dashboard, I refreshed the ads report and learned that it was Max Levchin, PayPal cofounder and *Thank You for Smoking* executive producer. Levchin had clicked the first time he had seen the ad: a 100 percent CTR.

The next click came from John Dickerson, *CBS News*'s political director and *Slate*'s chief political correspondent. I saw the blip appear over the Washington, D.C., metro on my blog's live visitor map, and I knew who it was before confirming my suspicions with the ad data. It was a bit like having a celebrity visiting your small town or neighborhood—you wonder what the person thinks of your modest patch of earth. Dickerson had seen the ad five times before clicking on the fifth impression: a 20 percent CTR.

The third click came from Nick Bilton, star columnist and *Bits* blogger for the *New York Times*. Bilton clicked the first time he saw it: another 100 percent CTR.

I knew why all of them had clicked on the ads: I caught their attention with a picture and a lie. The picture: a close-up on their face, found in a matter of seconds via Google Image Search. The copy in Max Levchin's ad read, "Max: Hire me! If I've earned your attention, click to learn why I should earn a job with you." John Dickerson's ad read, "John: I've got a story. It's perfect for Slate. Click to judge for yourself and contact me if it's a fit." Nick Bilton's ad was the same as Dickerson's. But I wasn't looking for a job, and I didn't have a story. I hoped they would forgive me when they learned that it wasn't a ploy, but rather a not-so-scientific experiment I created to answer two simple questions: Could Facebook ads be effectively targeted at individual business leaders and star journalists. And could I prove it? To find out, I had to be sure the ads stood out, hence my picture-and-lie strategy.

Facebook rolled out its Custom Audiences feature in 2012. It allows advertisers to target their existing databases of customers and prospects with display ads. By uploading contact data (e-mail, phone number, or Facebook user ID) to an application called Power Editor, ad managers can target specific users in their audience.[2] A ticket broker, for instance, could market tickets to an upcoming performance by displaying a Facebook ad to *only* those customers who had purchased tickets for that artist previously. An author could market her new book specifically to a segment of readers from an opt-in list she started upon launching her previous book. A business with a brand-new Facebook page could seamlessly acquire likes by promoting the page to its e-mail subscribers as they browsed Facebook—combining the right audience with the ideal context. In essence, this meant that advertisers no longer needed to rely on Facebook's targeting data for ad segmentation—they could bring their own. A custom audience is exactly the audience you want it to be, based on *your* data. This means a potentially massive increase in CTRs and user engagement. The Custom Audiences tool extended the power of e-mail and phone number lists beyond their natural channels and into the social web.

But what if you only care about reaching *one person*?

A few days before I created the ads that drew Levchin, Dickerson, and Bilton to my site, I posted something to my Facebook feed about another ads experiment I was running, and I asked friends for input. Mike Merrill replied with results of his own that, frankly, I found hard to believe at the time: a 75 percent CTR using Custom Audiences. By way of comparison, Facebook ads are doing exceptionally well if they net out at 2 percent CTR. Mike had been experimenting with completely customized, one-to-one ads to see if he could get his friends' attention. One of his tricks was to use an image of the friend in question; another was to use the friend's name in the headline. Even if people never pay attention to Facebook ads, they don't ignore their own face or name!

I had to try it. Mike introduced me to his friend Dennis Yu, CEO of BlitzMetrics. Yu was kind enough to give me a few tips and point me to some great resources he had written. The most surprising thing he told me? You can get *any* Facebook user's ID number from the URL of the person's profile, *regardless* of your friendship status or the person's privacy settings, with one simple trick. Just pull up a user's profile, chop off anything before Facebook.com in the URL, and replace it with "graph." Hit "Enter," and the number in the first line of text is the user ID. For example, my "vanity URL" is www .facebook.com/iangreenleigh, which you would change to graph.face-book.com/iangreenleigh to reveal my Facebook ID. (One advantage that IDs have over e-mail addresses is the fact that many people have more than one e-mail address, and the one you have may not be the one associated with the e-mail account the person uses to log in to Facebook. Not so with Facebook ID numbers; you cannot have more than one unless you have more than one Facebook account.)

Once that number is placed into a CSV spreadsheet and uploaded to Power Editor, a custom audience of one is ready for your ads. My first experiment was simple. I loaded a wedding photo into the ad builder and picked the headline, "Babe! Did this ad work?" My wife called a few hours after the ad was approved to say that it did. Now to take the loophole to its logical extreme.

All Facebook users are subject to the same ad targeting technology, but the difference in audience value between my wife and, say, Marissa Meyer isn't yet reflected in Facebook's fee scheme, which is built for big companies with big audiences and boatloads of cash to burn. Although Facebook charges $100 to message its founder, it would only cost about 20 *cents* to serve him your ad 1,000 times. That is a truly extraordinary imbalance.

Nick Bilton e-mailed me after he clicked on my ad, and he made a point I had considered at the beginning of this project:

*Your test is flawed because the only reason I clicked it was because
it freaked me out. So, I don't suspect anything like that will work
on me again.*

From my reply:

*The test was a proof of concept (the targeting, not the quality of
the ad) and not necessarily reliant on the creep factor. Although
in your case, I believe you that it wouldn't happen again or you
wouldn't have otherwise clicked on it. Anyway, sorry to bait and
switch.*

In other words, the test wasn't about the photo or the headline.
It was about the *ability* to reach any Facebook user. The proof was
in the click-through, matched to the ad data, and so the ad had to
stand out.

Ad data can drive you mad with speculation and anticipation.
Why isn't person A clicking on my clever ad? It has his face on it!
And when is person B going to get back on Facebook so I can test the
ad against more than a few impressions? I've always been interested
in testing and optimization, but individualized Custom Audiences
ads don't provide enough data from which to extract actionable con-
clusions. There's always a small chance that nothing you can do to
the ad will make it effective with your audience of one, which is why
your best bet is a dual approach: direct and indirect simultaneously.

Start by aiming one ad at your individual target. I've covered how
to do this already in this section. Run another aimed at colleagues
using this strategy. If your goal can be easily stated, like "Click to
see my résumé," place a call to action on your landing page that
instructs the visitor to contact your target on your behalf (this is
the strategy that worked in my LinkedIn campaign covered earlier).
For this ad type, bid on clicks, not impressions, since your landing
page is where the valuable action happens. Depending on a user's
privacy settings, you may be able to determine the Facebook IDs

of some of the person's Facebook friends. Concurrently, you can find third-party sources of information to learn the names and IDs of close colleagues and create ads specifically for them, as well. In some cases, Facebook can give you both data sets. For example, if I wanted to reach BuzzFeed founder Jonah Peretti, I'd pull up his profile and see that his friends list is public, as is a list of his friends "From Work," as determined by Facebook. To reach Peretti, I could create one ad just for him and one ad aimed at his colleagues. Or I could create one ad for him and a few one-to-one ads for his close colleagues. Either way, Custom Audiences will make sure the ads reach their targets.

Target Me, Please

Here's a fun test to see if you're doing it correctly. Target me! You can do it for free, unless your ad is so effective that I see it 1,000 times, at which point you'll be charged a whopping $0.10 to $0.50. Just follow these steps—it looks like a lot, but it's not.

What you'll need, besides Facebook:

- A Twitter profile or a page somewhere on the web with a contact form or e-mail address (so I can let you know I saw your ad)
- Microsoft Excel
- Google Chrome browser (not the mobile version)

The steps:

1. Pull up my profile: facebook.com/iangreenleigh.
2. Remove "https://www." Add "graph." It should look like this:

   graph.facebook.com/iangreenleigh

3. Hit "Enter," and copy the ID number on the first line with no quotes. It starts with 17.

4. Open up Excel. In cell A1 of a new document, paste the ID number from step 3. (Excel may try to convert the number into another format besides plain numbers, which will not work for our purposes. If this happens, format the cell as "Special" and select "Zip Code," and you'll have regular numbers again. It's weird, but it works.

5. Save the file as "Windows Comma Separate (.csv)." This is the only format that Facebook recognizes.

6. You'll need Chrome for the next few steps, so get it now if you don't have it. I'll wait.

7. Log in to Facebook, and go to www.Facebook.com/ads/manage.

8. If at any point during the next few steps Facebook asks you to download your accounts, do it without changing any of the default options.

9. Click "Power Editor" on the sidebar on the left.

10. Click "Custom Audience" on the sidebar on the left.

11. Click "Audiences" on the sidebar on the left.

12. Click "Create Audience" at the top.

13. Name the audience whatever you want, click "Choose File," and find the CSV you saved with my ID in it. Select "UIDs" from the "Type" options. Click "Create."

14. Click "Upload" on the top right.

15. Go back to www.Facebook.com/ads/manage. Hit "Create an Ad."

16. Enter the URL of the place where I can contact you (Twitter profile or contact page).

17. The copy can be whatever you want, as long as it contains the word *test*.

18. Find a photo of me. Try Google Image Search. Upload it to the ad builder.

19. Ignore all the targeting options except two. Select "United States," and select the custom audience from the check box. The audience size should shrink to <20.

20. From the bidding options, select "CPM." Bid at the top of the suggested range.
21. Create the ad and look for my signal!

Graph Search

As you might have noticed by now, I'm not big on intended uses. Facebook's Graph Search is marketed as a way to "find people who share your interests," "Discover restaurants, music and more," and "Explore your world through photos." These applications can be interesting, but Graph Search's true value emerges only when you read between the lines of Facebook's intended uses.

As we've discussed, Facebook's Custom Audiences feature is great for targeting users who are known to you. But Graph Search lets you find new people to get in front of using the same hypertargeted Custom Audiences system. What follows are several ways to use Graph Search as a social media side door by locating individuals to approach.

Want media coverage? Try "Friends of my friends who are currently reporters." Prefer coverage in your local market? "Reporters in Austin" (where I live) brings back more than 100 profiles. Are you connected to any of them through friends? "Friends of my friends who are currently reporters and live in Austin, Texas" yields six profiles and shows me how I'm connected.

National media can be found in the same manner. A search for "reporters who currently work at CNN" returns more than 100 people, and a search for "Producers who currently work at ABC News" returns 19 results.

You can also search by interest + job combinations. This is one of the ways I would pitch my book. For example, since I write about Facebook ads, I could pitch to some of the more than 1,000 "Reporters who like Facebook ads." To thin that number out, I can select by locale (United States) and time of employment as reporter (this year) to get down to around 100. In that group I found *Bloomberg Business* reporter Brian Womack and the *Verge* reporter Ellis Hamburger, both of whom had written about Facebook within the week. The search returned more than a few fakers and fictional jobs, too, such as the three users claiming to be reporters at the *Daily Planet* (just like Clark Kent).

Let's say you've got a book or an album to promote. Graph Search can help your visibility to prominent critics and review publications. Search by employer and fill in the blank with the outlets you'd like a review in: "People that currently work at _____." For example, searching for current *Publishers Weekly* employees yielded the profiles of several book reviewers, and doing the same for *Rolling Stone* located a handful of editors and reviewers. Maybe you're not signed yet, but you think your band is the next Florence and the Machine. Identify the 37 current Sony Music Entertainment employees who like Florence and the Machine and tell them that this is the chance for their label not to miss out again.

You get the idea by now. Unfortunately, Facebook does not make it easy to leverage Graph Search targeting efficiently. The most glaring functional weakness is the inability to import data from Graph Search searches into Facebook's ad products. This means that if you want to serve ads to the people you locate through Graph Search, you will need to manually add them to a custom audience. Another weakness, relative to LinkedIn, is that the job description field is an optional input for users and lacks category standardization (although there is some bleed-over between roles returned). Increasing Graph Search's usefulness will depend on people filling out information like this, but also sharing more of their favorite books, bands, movies, shows, and other interests to a degree many have not, and never will. On top of that, Graph Search does not support multiple queries for the same field in a given string. For example, you wouldn't be able to search "Reporters AND Producers who live in Austin, TX."

Graph Search is only in its infancy, and the future is promising. It's a framework that was built to support ads, so the advertising layer will roll out soon. The progression of ad technology follows a familiar pattern by now; many capabilities are released to corporate users and big accounts first, eventually opening up to users with smaller budgets (Twitter has done this with every ad type it releases).

- If you can't access someone directly, try to encourage his or her contacts to reach out on your behalf.
- The most effective ads are impossible to ignore—differentiate as much as possible from other elements on the page. Use humor, interesting imagery, segmentation, etc.
- Facebook's Custom Audiences feature allows advertisers to serve individualized ads to audiences of one. This little-known technique is very inexpensive.

CHAPTER 11

The Future of Access and Influence

The access we have to one another today through social media will bewilder people five years from now. More precisely, the *ways* we access one another will seem comparatively primitive, open to exploitation and abuse. It will be the digital equivalent of "Can you believe we used to leave our doors unlocked all night in this neighborhood?" And yet as the history of communications demonstrates so vividly, access never really goes away. It just sets up shop down the block.

The democratization of influence is unstoppable. Our idols are no longer assigned to us; we choose them for ourselves. Tribes and tribalism, long the entrenched enemies of progress, persist and in many ways are stronger than ever. But this expanding social universe consists of tribes who are united by common interest, not just proximity, class, creed, race, and fear of the other. The ties holding them together are weaker, often ephemeral. But they are more agile, more transcendent, and frequently more powerful than the tribes of the past. And so are their leaders. These tribes don't tolerate nepotism, kingmaking, or external manipulation; influence, and thus lead-ership, is accrued over time (the devoted blogger or forum points leader) or is suddenly achieved (the overnight YouTube sensation).

At Long Last

This is the moment in time so many of us have been waiting for. If what you create doesn't have mass-market appeal, you're not doomed to obscurity and failure. Seth Godin is as exhilarated by this as I am:

> *You are chaos, and there is nothing to keep you out. When network engineers think about the security of the network, they begin with a firewall. The firewall is designed to keep unwanted information and viruses out of the system. The Internet doesn't have a firewall. We're all able to connect. We each represent the ghost in the machine, the noise, the one who might change every-thing. What you feed the network changes what you get back. The network connects people to one another, people to organizations, and best of all, people to ideas. This new network celebrates art, enables connections, helps tribes to form, amplifies weirdness, and spreads ideas. What it cannot abide is boredom.*

You can now succeed, instead, by reaching the relative few who care, because they're just a few nodes away on a real-time global network. You can exchange value—and values—with people you will *never* meet in the physical world, and yet these relationships can be every bit as meaningful and rewarding as they were when "knowing" people meant having engaged with them in person.

In "Game Over," a radio piece on NPR's *Snap Judgment*, one such community, The Sims Online, is eulogized. Why would a game be eulogized? Because it was shut down by Electronic Arts, and with it, a social universe was erased. It was a "place" where people went simply to connect. "Over time, it became like an intimate . . . almost

... bar—like the Cheers of video games," recalls Robert Ashley. For Paul Monaco, who had recently lost his wife to hepatitis C, The Sims Online "was kind of a way for me to get back into living again." Says Roman Mars, host of the radio show 99% *Invisible*, "It wasn't the real world, but his friends were real friends."

As the clock counted down to the end of the *Sims* world, its importance as a social destination, along with the depth of the relationships it fostered, was vividly captured in the interactions of the social game's players. Players wept and exchanged sorrowful farewells, and then the digital "end" arrived. Its players, a close-knit clan of friendly people from all over the physical world, were left without a digital world of their own to inhabit. So they found other places to connect, like YouTube—and the physical world.

Paul Monaco made the most out of the social skills he picked up in the game and ventured out into other realms, according to a comment on one of his YouTube videos: "Loving my tweet-ups and podcamps with real interaction between the pixelated and carbon world."[1]

I've found a similar fulfillment; I'm amazed by how the digital and physical frequently lead to one another and by how the two are being woven together into a richer experience than either could offer on its own.

Disappearing Barriers

I happened to catch the beginning of what would unfold into a thoughtful exploration of the disappearing barriers between modes of experience (which is not as heady as it sounds). It started as a request in a tweet from Erin Kissane, an editor and content strategist:

I need terms for distinguishing the digital from the . . . not digital.[2]

Dozens of others recognized the same need and chimed in with suggestions, ranging from "offline" to "corporeal," and the difficulty arriving at a consensus illustrated a larger point: describing the edges between the ways we experience the world is challenging because, increasingly, those edges don't seem to exist. When "in real life" was proposed, Kissane's response hit the mark:

> But things that happen via the digital nevertheless happen. They are real. Which is why "IRL" is so maddening.[3]

Increasingly, online is not somewhere you *go*; it's something you *are*. Technology has always played its role in escaping reality, but it has also always helped shape reality. Aside from academics and authors like me, most people don't spend time thinking about the borders between their own experiences; they simply transcend them as they live their lives. They tweet while watching TV; they read reviews from their smartphone in the store aisle; they work from home and Skype into meetings. None of these remarkably converged experiences are costly, nor do they require much technical knowledge. They don't feel particularly revolutionary unless you stop and think about them. In fact, the only time most people think about the edges between things is when they obstruct them in some way, like "Why can't I just print pictures from my camera wirelessly?" or "Why can't I watch this on my phone?"

Seeing the Side Doors

Similarly, people tend not to think about their own access and influence in such a deliberate way. Doing so seems somewhat unnatural, like a needless self-examination that gets in the way of "real life." One of the reasons I've written this book is to help people understand that thinking about their own access and influence actually *enriches* life. When we start to see side doors everywhere, or the makings of them, we can take advantage of opportunities that others don't notice. But it's an acquired way of seeing the world, not a natural ability. There are edges between people, too. Too often they are barriers to communication, meaningful relationships, efficiency, and progress. We're trained to see these barriers and to *believe* in their impenetrability. In many cases, we're told that it's wisest not to approach them at all; better to stick to what we know, whom we can access, and what we can achieve. It takes some mental rewiring to see barriers as the dusty artifacts and hole-ridden fences they have become.

When I tell people that I took out a Facebook ad to find a job, the number one response is, "I didn't know you could do that!" A friend of mine, a soldier about to transition into civilian life, told me, "I didn't even know that type of social media existed." He and my other friends who have served or are serving in the military use social media more than any other group I know. To them, it's a line home, and later it's a connection to that important kinship with others in their unit, now scattered stateside. If anyone can use social media to advance in life, it's power users like them. But for the most part, they do not. Social media and upward mobility don't typically intersect in life, so the true extent of the *potential* and *proven* relationship between the two is unknown to the vast majority of social media users, as well as power users like these guys.

The New Norms of Access

I started thinking about the topic of side doors knowing that things would be different by the time I was finished with this book. The "social media for job seekers" topic has gone mainstream. I'm being asked to guest-lecture to business students more and more, and dedicated classes are being offered in social media marketing at colleges all around the world. World leaders, CEOs, and even the papacy have flocked to Twitter. Every résumé I see lists social media skills and experience. The conversation *about* social media is starting to catch up to the ways people use social media. As social networks reach the remote corners of the world and as previously closed societies like Burma join the fray, the social web reflects the world we live in more accurately. These societies will soon enjoy an unprecedented degree of openness.

People are just waking up to the new norms of access; soon they will simply expect them. They will find it odd not to have access to the thoughts, musings, and unscripted words of public figures. They will be skeptical or dismissive of both those who have no social media presence and those who have shut themselves off from all access. In much the same way that Americans value the right to petition their government, many will view *access* to people, brands, and institutions *as a kind of right.* Four years ago, governmental blocking of social networks may have seemed like a relatively minor affront compared with the myriad instruments of oppression employed by regimes around the world. But in the wake of the Arab Spring and the conflict in Syria, where social media has been a *vital* lifeline—indeed, a matter of life and death—the cruelty in this form of censorship is seen in a new light.

The Enablers Awaken

The access enablers understand the value of what they provide, and they are starting to act a lot like gatekeepers—or more precisely, tollbooth operators. Facebook has changed the way it displays brand page content in users' timelines, favoring content from paying advertisers. As a result, brands are finding it more difficult to reach sizable audiences without shelling out for them. Advertising rates are skyrocketing year over year. Facebook and its advertisers see access as contextual. Showing ads to users browsing from laptop or desktop computers is providing access to users in one specific context. But people live more of their lives in "mobile mode," even within their homes. Users spend more time browsing Facebook from mobile devices than from desktop computers, and mobile advertising jumped from 14 to 23 percent of Facebook's revenue in just one quarter.[4, 5] Advertisers want access to desired audiences in every context, and the mobile context is a newer, largely unconquered frontier. This is why advertisers are bidding higher for mobile ads and spending more of their budgets on this context.[6] If users are Facebooking from the bathroom, as one-third of Americans are, advertisers would like to reach them there as well.[7] There is no limit to the appetite for access.

Facebook's update to its message delivery system is indicative of the changes to come. It has been the case that messages sent to non-friends end up in the "Other" in-box (sort of a junk mail folder that users rarely check), and they don't trigger a normal message alert within Facebook or via e-mail. Now, a system is being piloted in 40 countries that lets users pay to skip the "Other" slush pile and send their messages directly to the regular in-box of someone with whom they're not connected.[8] Pricing is variable, based on factors such as geography as well as "the popularity of the person you're trying to contact and how many other messages are sent their way."[9] Facebook justifies the system by claiming that "paying to reach someone you aren't connected to helps confirm your message isn't spam." To reach Mark Zuckerberg, nonfriends are charged $100 per message. Getting a message to Salman Rushdie will run users about $16.50.

Twitter, too, is betting that brands will be willing to pay for access to wider and more targeted audiences. Its ad products take the form of favored placement of content and accounts to targeted audiences. Twitter Promoted Tweets are featured in timelines and search results in the web and mobile apps. These tweets can be targeted to users who have tweeted certain keywords, users in specific geographies, people tweeting in specific languages, and users who are determined by Twitter to *resemble* specific accounts (known as look-alike targeting) or to share a limited array of interests. Interestingly, Twitter has not provided targeting features that allow advertisers to target specific accounts. This ability is conspicuously absent, though no doubt technically achievable, which signals that Twitter is being very deliberate about how, when, and at what cost it rolls out what is probably its trump card.

Twitter Promoted Trends artificially boost the visibility of sponsored hashtags. Promoted Accounts appear prominently in users' search results and in Twitter's "Who to Follow" recommendations. All these options reflect a market for access to audiences just as much as they reflect a market for *perceived* influence. If one is paying to appear in the "Who to Follow" results, one is essentially paying for followers and for the perceived influence that comes with a high follower count. Not coincidentally, those little blue check marks that denote "Verified Accounts" are available only to "highly sought users" (celebrities and well-known brands) and "business partners" (paid advertisers).[10] These symbols are ostensibly meant to prove authenticity—that Twitter users are who they say they are—but they are coveted as a kind of "official" stamp of social proof. They indicate that those bearing check marks are influential. Anecdotally, I gather that individuals do not experience a discernible spike in followers after receiving the badge. As my friend Brian Cuban wrote, "I was the same old guy. Tweeting, arguing, blocking, getting blocked and being a general douche at times when people annoy me."[11] I can testify that he's telling the truth.

LinkedIn's ad model leans heavily on its supergranular data, but like Facebook, it has begun to charge for higher levels of access. Premium users can see full profiles for more users in their network, receive information about who is viewing their *own* profile, ask for "warm introductions" from more mutual contacts, and send direct "InMail" messages to "gain access to decision-makers." LinkedIn is confident that its premium InMail feature will help users access the hard to reach; it guarantees responses within seven days. LinkedIn Recruiter is a productized suite of features designed to help recruiters find "passive candidates" (those not actively looking for, but open to, new opportunities); it's marketed as a service that "expands your access" to full names and profiles over the entire network and to granular recruiter-friendly data, and it provides a subscription to InMail.

It's hard to say which network's model looks more like the future, but they share a common underlying belief that reaching people, from audiences in the millions to single candidates, is something that many users will pay for. For most users, this is the future of social media, access, and influence: preference for those that pay.

The desire for access and influence via social media is so palpable that it has spawned its own thriving black market, the largest of which surrounds Twitter. One can buy Twitter followers in bulk from countless vendors, in direct violation of Twitter's terms of service. The market has become so saturated that competition between vendors no longer hinges on the ratio of followers to price; some will claim that "their" followers will stick with you for a year or more; some will claim to broker "real" followers (as opposed to bots), and the list goes on. Some Twitter accounts claim to broker verified account status by posing as official Twitter entities. This scam tapped into a vein of desire among Twitter users, and as the *Verge* reports, the results of one such instance are telling:

> *It was a good run for fake Twitter account @privateverified, which was just suspended after earning more than 22,000 followers in under 24 hours by pretending to issue the blue check marks that denote verified Twitter accounts. Its first tweet, "#RT if i Should Verified Your Accounts," got 6,440 retweets and 693 favorites, mostly from users who probably would not qualify for the elite designation.[12]*

While the motivations of the above scammer aren't clear (the person did not ask for money), the desire among users of social networks for recognition of influence and access to wider audiences could not be more obvious. Facebook likes can be bought just like Twitter followers. Paid "systems" abound that purportedly help people game their Klout scores. Third-party scam operators and the networks themselves are both trying to monetize the same things: access and influence (and the related status and benefits that come with each).

They Can't Shut It Down

The social networks are trying to control the distribution of access and influence just enough to exploit them as revenue streams. But the networks will never completely take away these resources from nonpaying users. The networks realize that if everyday users don't believe that they can earn them organically, the loyalty of the users will end. Every so often, users will see a high-profile user engage with someone like them, an "average" user, and they'll be hooked once again. They'll want the same access, the shout-out, the follow, the share, or something more substantial. They'll see that a blog post can ruin a company's reputation and that positive reviews can help small businesses shine brighter than big competitors with advertising budgets.

Social media will cease to exist as we know it if it stops providing a means to access and influence. Without access, there is no connection. Without influence, connections have no value. The continued growth and success of social media *requires* that people always see it as an opportunity to leave a mark, to be noticed, to connect with the elite—all in ways that are impossible through other media. When I first began to ponder the ideas that would become this book, I thought of democratized influence and ungated access as a subset of peculiar features in a landscape brimming with fascinating features and dynamics (among them: pokes, comments, untagging, Redditors, selfies, hashtags, going viral). But soon after, I realized that influence and access *are* the social media landscape. These ideas are central to the experience. There is no social media without them.

Reflecting once more on the nature of these social media side doors, I return again and again to an image of an impossibly long line. It's made up of people from every walk of life, and it hasn't moved in hours. Some appear restless; some seem bored; some are lost in thought, imagining whatever it is on the other side of the door. It doesn't matter what it is. It could be anything. What matters is that everyone in this line wants it. Near the middle of the line stands a woman who would blend right into the crowd if it weren't for the direction of her gaze. The people in the rest of the line are looking ahead, eyes fixed on the door that marks their destination but never seems to open. But she's looking backward, toward the beginning of the line. Back there, she was optimistic, even excited. She had a plan—she was finally on her way. Now, having reached the halfway mark, she expected to feel as though she'd accomplished *something*. But the expression on her face tells another story. She contemplates her situation for a few moments and then gives up her place in line. Others stare at her as she walks past them, puzzled about why she would abandon a position in line they're nowhere near reaching themselves. She can't bear the unwanted attention any longer, so she decides in the moment to duck into an unassuming alley, hoping the detour will lead her back home, eventually. Walking quickly, she passes by an unmarked door. "I'm sure it's locked," she thinks to herself. And then she stops, turns around, and tries the handle anyway.

I try not to wonder what my life would be like if I hadn't followed through after reading that blog post about Facebook ads for job seekers. It meant stepping outside of my comfort zone and taking a chance on something that, deep down, I didn't think would probably work. If anything in this book strikes you—even for a nanosecond— as worth a shot, you owe it to yourself to take it. And if you learn of a potential social media side door hidden in plain sight, fight the temptation to immediately lock it behind you. Leave it open, and you'll be amazed at the people, ideas, and opportunities that walk right in.

Tools and Techniques

Don't believe people who tell you they have a single solution to all your social media needs—they're selling snake oil. The landscape is just too new—and in too much chaos—for one-size-fits-all applications to be effective. Success in this realm is achieved by way of an evolving patchwork of solutions, unique to one's needs and aspirations. It doesn't need to be expensive or complicated or rudimentary. It just needs to work *for you*.

I've personally used everything in this section while charting my path through the social media universe, and I recommend trying all of them yourself. Most of the tools and services are free or low cost for basic functionality, and they are for personal or single-user needs (many offer enterprise-level plans as well).

I wish I had a magic way to ensure that all the tools I'm about to describe are still running and accessible when you're reading this. I don't. One thing I've discussed again and again throughout these pages is the crumbling of barriers to entry, and that applies to tools and businesses, too. Something that has been created with just a little time, skill, and capital may prove useful to you and me, but it may not turn out to be as viable a business as its creator had initially hoped. The social web is littered with 404 pages, GoDaddy placeholders, and abandoned ghost towns where seriously nifty tools—and even entire communities—once resided. And a lot of companies have been snapping up smaller social media outfits, hungry for their technology, talent, user base, data, and clients. Consolidation of this kind usually means free or cheap services are discontinued or wrapped into far pricier offerings. But those absurdly low entry costs mean that by the time you're reading this, hundreds of powerful tools I could never have predicted are available to you.

Please know that no one is compensating me for including any offerings in this section.

And please share your discoveries of new and refreshed tools and services with other readers (and me!) by tweeting them along with the official hashtag of this book, #tsmsd.

A few general tips:

- If you try something and you don't think you'll use it again in the foreseeable future, make sure to revoke its access to your social profiles and data. You can change app access settings to your Twitter profile by signing in, selecting settings from the gear icon menu at the top, and then clicking "Apps" on the sidebar. On Facebook, sign in and select "App Settings" from the gear icon menu at the top and then select "Apps" from the sidebar.

- One of the first things you should do upon signing up for one of these services is to head to the e-mail settings page to make sure your in-box won't be flooded with stuff you don't want or need.

- Don't fall victim to the two most distracting digital ailments of our time: *shiny object syndrome* (SOS), and *fear of missing out* (FOMO). Sign up for tools and services only because they look like they can help you, not because they are hot. I fall for this thinking as much as anyone else, but I'm working on it. You can spread yourself too thin and wear yourself out if you feel the need to post everywhere all the time. You'll also—inevitably—leave a trail of "ghost" profiles that don't reflect the best of you (or much of anything). Delete or deactivate as soon as you know it's not for you. Regarding FOMO, it will never completely go away. If you're anything like me, there will always be that tugging feeling: "Should I be doing that?" The question to ask to minimize distractions is, "Should I give up some of what I'm doing now to do that?" The answer is usually no. You may indeed miss out, but pursuing option B over option A doesn't always make sense in terms of opportunity cost.

Now, get to it!

Refollow

Trim the Fat from Your Twitter Network

If you want good content and great conversations, you'll need to use a tool like Refollow as your network expands. A free account lets you bulk-analyze the accounts of people you follow for activity levels, following-to-followers ratios, interaction histories, reciprocity—whether they follow you or not—and more. Like most third-party tools, Refollow is subject to limited API calls to Twitter, so the analysis isn't instant. I personally use Refollow to display users whom I follow but who don't follow me, and then I sort by last tweet to bulk-unfollow those who are inactive. (One of the bitter truths is that following-to-follower ratios matter to some, usually as a quick heuristic for analyzing the size of someone's social impact.)

FIND IT: refollow.com

Buffer

Fill and Optimize Your Content Pipeline

I'm prone to bursts of social activity. If I have 30 minutes of downtime, I might read and share a few articles within that window. But if this takes place at a time when my friends and followers aren't listening, it's a tree-falls-in-the-woods situation. I don't advocate automating most or all of your social presence, since it leaves no room for organic interaction, but I do think it is important to keep activity levels up and to monitor when your posts are most effective. Buffer helps you easily add content to your social post pipeline from your desktop browser or mobile device, and it optimizes your schedule by posting when your network is most active. It integrates with Twitter, Facebook, and LinkedIn, and it lets you calibrate timing for each network independently. It's great to have a single tool to share the great content you find across the web with users on each of your networks—all in a few clicks. The analytics on the back end track clicks and other data, and they help users understand when and why content hits or misses. All around, one of the best free tools out there to help individuals build influence through content curation.

FIND IT: bufferapp.com

followerwonk

Compare Accounts and Learn More About Your Followers

This is a Twitter user comparison and network analysis service that compiles a ton of revealing data. You can have it analyze your own account to learn high-level things about your followers, such as gender breakdown, activity and engagement levels, account age, peak hours, and much more. Through a more granular lens, followerwonk can be used to compare yourself with any nonprivate Twitter user to identify common contacts (always a good starting point for engagement). The paid version also offers a way to identify your most influential followers, as judged by followerwonk's proprietary influence score or through a limited number of metrics like follower count. This feature is useful because once follower counts start climbing, key follows can easily slip through the cracks. For example, I was surprised (and pleased) to learn that *Forbes* magazine, followed by more than 1.2 million users, follows me and only about

350 others. That's a potentially gigantic social media side door that I would have completely missed if I hadn't been using quality tools.

FIND IT: followerwonk.com

Topsy

Gauge the Social Reach of Your Content

Topsy is one of the most underrated and underutilized free tools out there. I've been rather spoiled at Bazaarvoice when it comes to access to expensive analytics tools, but I happily admit that Topsy's free offering has rivaled the power of costly tools like Critical Mention when it comes to its evaluation of reach. Pop a URL (or any text) into the search field, and you'll see a list of social posts that contain it and its popularity trended over time, sortable by the influence of the accounts posting it. Topsy, unlike many popular paid tools, looks *behind* shortened URLs and matches to characters in the original (long) URL. This is really important because Twitter.com and most third-party Twitter clients use URL shorteners to conserve space within the 140-character limit, and the character string you search for from the original URL will not appear in the shortened version. Here's a common example. Say someone tweets something like this about your latest blog post:

Love this post! I want to hire this guy! www.exampleurl.com/xyz.

Twitter and services like TweetDeck take that URL and change it to something condensed, like bit.ly/VkTdNy. Topsy will still return the latter version as a hit, even though it no longer contains the full URL or term you're searching for, and this cannot be said of countless competing tools out there. No matter which search tool you use to track your impact on the social web, make sure it offers this feature.

FIND IT: topsy.com

Storify

Quickly Curate the World Around You

One of my favorite strategies for opening social media side doors is to be among the first to cover something. This is the thinking that led to the huge traffic payoff when @nytcomm (an official *New York Times* account) tweeted a link to a recap post I wrote about one of the sessions given by the *Times* at a conference I was attending; I published the piece first, so I was the most visible among conference-goers who wrote about the talk.

Storify is a simple, inclusive way to recap events or social conversations quickly, with a few unique social media side doors written right into the code. Users create "stories" by patching together social content and their own commentary into a single, visually appealing thread. Use its powerful search feature to find tweets, blog excerpts, pictures, and videos from around the social web; then weave them together to tell a story. Your story can be embedded on your own blog or site with just a few clicks. I've tried nearly every curation tool out there, and the social notification elements set Storify apart: when you publish a story, all the content sources can be instantly notified of their inclusion. Once you share it, chances are they'll share it. Ego capital at work! For one of the best examples out there, check out the way the *Los Angeles Times* covered the February 2013 shocking car chase and shoot-out in Las Vegas: lat.ms/WZsgm6.

FIND IT: storify.com

ClickToTweet

The Convenience of Auto-Population—Embedded Anywhere

Most of the Twitter share plug-ins for blogs use auto-population, which means that when you click the tweet button, it will prefill the content of your tweet with the title of the post, a shortened link, and the author's name or Twitter handle (usually formats vary). But these buttons usually exist at the top or bottom of a post; their content is meant to describe the entire post. What if you want to embed a call to tweet something unique from within your post (not just at the beginning and end)? For example, if you're writing a "Top 10 Quotes by Nas" post, each quote could be tweeted individually just by clicking on a nearby link, and the content of those tweets would be prefilled with the quote, a link back to the post, and the Twitter handle or name of its source, like this:

> *My first album had no famous guest appearances / The outcome: I'm crowned the best lyricist.—@Nas*

All you need to do is fill in the text you want and enter the URL to be shortened, and you're set. Another ego capital optimization courtesy of a reliable, free tool. (I'm not so sure Nas needs another ego boost, referring to himself in his album as God's Son and all, but you get the larger point.)

FIND IT: clicktotweet.com

If This Then That

Be the First to Know

There are thousands of interesting ways to use If This Then That (IFTTT), a service that helps users tie together technologies that don't normally integrate without complicated work-arounds. Some of the most popular "recipes," as the automated mash-ups are called, are simple: "When Facebook profile picture changes, update Twitter profile picture." "Text me the weather every morning." Things like that. I like to use IFTTT to instantly alert me about things like new posts from my favorite bloggers, which allows me to be among the first readers to comment. There are a few ways to do this, but here's a relatively simple one. Create a new folder in Google Reader, and add to it the feeds of some of the bloggers you're trying to get in front of. Sign up for IFTTT and create your first recipe. For the "trigger channel," select Google Reader, and approve the integration. Next, select "New item tagged," and enter the exact name of the folder you created in Google Reader. Now you can choose how you would prefer to be alerted—by SMS, e-mail, etc. Alternatively, if you want to set up individual alerts for bloggers without using Google Reader, just use the "feed" trigger item, and you'll be alerted whenever the blogger of your choice posts something new.

FIND IT: ifttt.com

Twitter Lists and Columns
Focus Your Access Efforts, Preserve Your Ratio

Lists are a popular native Twitter feature that allows you to organize users into groups of your choice. Lists can be private or public, and every third-party Twitter client I know of lets you filter or display activity by list, and many of the apps let you do this by column. It's helpful to create lists of people based on interest or access level. For example, I have a list dedicated to media outlets and reporters, which appears as a column in my TweetDeck dashboard. I also have a private list of influencers I'd like to get to know personally, and this appears as another column. This allows me to keep up with breaking news and the latest updates from my influencers without having to dig through barrages of tweets from everyone I follow. I set goals to engage with a few people on my influencers list every day, and it's very rewarding to see the effect this has over time on my access to the people on the list. Another appealing aspect of lists is that they make it possible to keep up with accounts without following them. If an account only updates occasionally or doesn't follow people back, it makes more sense to add it to a list than to follow it. Doing so doesn't impact your following-to-follower ratio negatively, and you'll see the account's updates just as you would if you were following it.

FIND TWITTER LIST FEATURE: twitter.com → Me → Lists

FIND TWEETDECK: TweetDeck.com

Twitter List Copy

Big Flexibility in a Small Package

You'll often want to build your lists from another user's list as a starting point. Problem is, Twitter does not let you alter a list you've subscribed to. Noah Liebman created a simple, no-frills tool that addresses this lack in native functionality by allowing you to copy lists from other users and make them your own.

FIND IT: bit.ly/VbwMxL

Twitter Question Search

Discover Opportunities to Be Helpful

This is a native search feature of Twitter.com that delivers only tweets containing any variable (word, phrase, hashtag, language, user, place, etc.) *and* a question. For example, searching for #SXSW questions, I found a tweet from the *Wall Street Journal* asking for bar and restaurant tips for the SXSW festival; responding to a tweet like this is a great opportunity to get noticed by a major outlet.

FIND IT: twitter.com/search-advanced

TweetChat

Managed Chaos

I've probably recommended this free hashtag-based chat tool more than any other social media tool in my career. Whether you're trying to monitor breaking news or participate in a real-time chat (like #blogchat), TweetChat will enhance and manage the experience. With TweetChat you can:

1. Get real-time updates for any hashtag within focused stream
2. Adjust update speed, pause stream

3. Block, highlight users
4. Automatically have your hashtags appended to posts
5. Temporarily filter out retweets to see only originals

FIND IT: tweetchat.com

What the Trend

Discover Trends

What the Trend tracks and ranks trending hashtags, makes them searchable, and allows users to place them in context by adding definitions. It also offers a few cool reports, like top Twitter trends of the past 30 days and a list of the spammiest hashtags.

FIND IT: wthashtag.com

Trendsmap

The World According to Twitter

This tool visualizes popular hashtags by location (city, country) to detect regional trends, and it also identifies globally trending users.

FIND IT: trendsmap.com

Facebook Ads

Basic

Despite the rising cost, Facebook ads can still be an incredible investment. Target by employer, likes, geography, and more. Run multiple variants to optimize over time. I suggest creating simple, custom landing pages to tailor your messages to those clicking the ad. Throw in a nice picture and a snappy call to action, and you've got yourself a killer social media side door.

FIND IT: on.fb.me/XDNO7w

Facebook Ads

Promoted Page Posts

If you have a Facebook page (as opposed to profile), this is a good option for you. Promoted Page posts place your posts in the timelines of nonfans who are connected to your fans. The way I do it is kind of like the way a comic tries out jokes on smaller crowds before bringing them to the big stage. I'll post something to my page organically, and I'll assess the response. If it gets an above-average response, I click the "Promote" button near the bottom, commit $5 to it, and watch the links and shares accumulate. This feature doesn't give you much control over targeting (let's just say I have a strangely high number of page fans from former Soviet nations in Central Asia), but it takes advantage of the network effect wonderfully.

MORE INFO: on.fb.me/12cnshg

Facebook Ads

Custom Audiences

Of all the social media side door strategies in the book, I dare say Custom Audiences has the best ROI, so much so that I'm legitimately curious about whether Facebook itself knows what can be done with it! *Take advantage of this feature soon.*

To summarize, Custom Audiences lets you upload a list of e-mail addresses, phone numbers, or Facebook unique IDs and target *only* the profiles associated with that list. For example, a ticket broker could market tickets to an upcoming performance by displaying a Facebook ad to only those customers who had purchased tickets for that artist previously.

But the *real trick* is one-to-one targeting. It's how I served up unique ads to Yahoo CEO Marissa Meyer and how I got clicks from PayPal cofounder Max Levchin, *CBS News*'s John Dickerson, and star *New York Times* columnist Nick Bilton. Everyone on Facebook has a unique ID, and you can figure out what it is regardless of the person's privacy settings or your friend or not-friend status (see Chapter 10).

FIND IT: www.facebook.com/ads/manage → Power Editor → Custom Audiences

Facebook Graph Search

Find Facebook Users

Graph Search can help you find Facebook users that match criteria you're searching for. A few example searches:

- Friends of my friends who are currently reporters
- Reporters who currently work at CNN
- Sony Music Entertainment employees who like Florence and the Machine

Currently, there is no way to export these users into Excel or Custom Audiences, so I'd call Graph Search a cool proof of concept to keep an eye on.

MORE INFO: www.facebook.com/about/graphsearch

LinkedIn Ads

Target Specific Job Functions and Seniority Levels

These ads can be targeted by many of the same fields as Facebook ads, but they offer better precision targeting by specific job functions and seniority levels. I set up these ads as if I were a job seeker with Google and Facebook in mind. I found 1,428 LinkedIn members by using the following string: "US residents age 25 or older who work in Marketing or Media and Communication at Google as a Director, Manager, Senior (X), VP, or C(X)O." LinkedIn's suggested bid range was $2.14–$2.26 per click or $2.14–$2.26 per 1,000 impressions.

When I tried the same string for Facebook as the workplace, the string didn't return enough members to qualify. I tried removing the job function (Marketing or Media and Communication), and that worked; I met the minimum scope, and the bid prices were exactly the same as the Google variant. One of the benefits of LinkedIn ads over Facebook ads is the professional context in which users see them. It's hard to quantify the edge that gives these ads, but it's generally a good idea to approach people through a vehicle that reflects your desired relationship with them in addition to more social channels like Facebook and Twitter.

FIND IT: linkedin.com/ads/

LinkedIn Premium

Make Direct Contact

This service isn't free, and that's a good thing, since it would be exploited to death and shut down in a matter of days if it were. Premium lets you make direct contact with nearly any LinkedIn user through InMail, expands search capabilities, and lets you see who's been looking at your profile. I've been able to contact several people through InMail who had shut themselves off to access through most other means. I suggest subscribing only during months in which you have a lot of outreach planned, or else the fee might not be worth it.

FIND IT: linkd.in/ZKcVs4

Muck Rack

Get Social with 15,000 Journalists and Bloggers

To get the most out of this tool, you'll need to purchase a paid subscription. Muck Rack is great for a number of reasons:

- Finding the right journalists (including bloggers) to approach

- Discovering which hot topics are trending among journalists
- Providing links to journalists' social profiles
- Offering individualized instructions for pitching
- Sending out keyword alerts that notify you when journalists are discussing the keywords of your choice

FIND IT: muckrack.com

NOTES

CHAPTER 1

1. techcrunch.com/2011/03/13/twitters-beginning/
2. www.referenceforbusiness.com/businesses/G-L/Lucent-Technologies .html#b
3. www.pbs.org/wgbh/nova/time/through2.html
4. www.oldtelephonebooks.com/pbnh.html
5. en.wikipedia.org/wiki/Timeline_of_the_telephone
6. www.pbs.org/fmc/book/15communication5.htm
7. directmag.com/history/birth-telemarketing/
8. inventors.about.com/od/astartinventions/a/Answering.htm
9. www.radicati.com/wp/wp-content/uploads/2011/05/Email-Statistics -Report-2011-2015-Executive-Summary.pdf
10. indigenoustweets.com/
11. en.wikipedia.org/wiki/Diffusion_of_Innovations
12. www.mediabistro.com/alltwitter/files/2012/07/fortune-500-ceos-social.jpeg
13. www.mediabistro.com/alltwitter/the-us-has-the-most-twitter-users-but -the-netherlands-is-more-active-stats_b18172
14. www.radicati.com/wp/wp-content/uploads/2011/05/Email-Statistics -Report-2011-2015-Executive-Summary.pdf
15. en.wikipedia.org/wiki/Advertising_adstock
16. www.ajr.org/article.asp?id=530
17. www.nytimes.com/2012/03/17/us/justice-department-investigation-is -sought-in-florida-teenagers-shooting-death.html?_r=1
18. m.npr.org/news/Technology/149048259?page=1
19. kantarmediana.com/intelligence/press/us-advertising-expenditures -increased-3-percent-2012
20. www.marketingcharts.com/wp/television/are-young-people-watching-less -tv-24817/
21. money.cnn.com/2011/04/15/technology/ebooks_beat_paperbacks/index.htm
22. allthingsd.com/20130129/amazons-ebook-business-is-up-70-percent-but -its-still-not-disclosing-kindle-sales/

23. www.mediabistro.com/fishbowlny/nick-denton-says-gawkers-standards
-of-publication-are-lower_b55224
24. www.nytimes.com/2010/07/19/business/media/19press.html?pagewanted
=all&_r=0
25. iq.intel.com/story/8513442/iq-a-new-publishing-model-1
26. www.mpdailyfix.com/seven-reasons-your-content-marketing-needs-a
-brand-journalist/
27. twitter.com/#!/copyblogger/statuses/129283089057853440

CHAPTER 2

1. content.usatoday.com/communities/driveon/post/2011/07/nearly-17000
-show-up-to-try-for-ford-jobs-in-louisville/1
2. www.bls.gov/web/jolts/jlt_labstatgraphs.pdf
3. www.independent.co.uk/news/education/education-news/graduate-gloom
-as-83-apply-for-every-vacancy-2303650.html
4. www.mediapost.com/publications/article/134553/
5. daretocomment.com/what-klout-cant-calculate/#comment-9
6. paidcontent.org/2013/01/24/new-york-times-editor-to-take-75000-twitter
-followers-out-the-door-with-him/
7. socialmedia.iceable.com/2011/12/16/twitter-the-new-resume/
8. mashable.com/2013/01/14/ad-agency-linkedin-bomb/
9. tomglocer.com/blogs/default.aspx
10. www.saatchi.com/en/global_network/clients
11. careers.guardian.co.uk/careers-blog/advertising-industry-job-applications
12. www.guerrillacheesemarketing.com/2012/02/29/guerrilla-marketing-the
-facebook-job-experiment-saatchi-saatchi-la/
13. krconnect.blogspot.com/
14. online.wsj.com/article/SB10001424052970203479104577125403745409234
.html
15. www.huffingtonpost.com/2011/10/06/larry-ellison-marc-benioff-oracle
-openworld_n_998604.html
16. blog.marketo.com/blog/2011/10/how-to-catalyze-a-pr-win-into-revenue
-with-marketing.html
17. en.wikipedia.org/wiki/Sunk_costs#Loss_aversion_and_the_sunk_cost
_fallacy
18. www.brainyquote.com/quotes/keywords/ideas_2.html#ixzz1i3YfyfnT
19. badpitch.blogspot.com/2010/01/will-facebook-ad-land-pr-job-seeker-his
.html
20. community.forrester.com/message/9445#9445
21. www.forrester.com/2011+Now+Social+Media+Marketing+Gets+Tough
/fulltext/-/E-RES57771?objectid=RES57771
22. hbr.org/hbrg-main/resources/pdfs/ad-sales/hbr-dedicated-readers-booklet
.pdf

23. www.briansolis.com/2011/02/when-will-the-social-media-gatekeepers -arrive/
24. blogs.hbr.org/cs/2010/12/six_social_media_trends_for_20_1.html
25. daretocomment.com/the-little-blog-comment-that-made-it-into-the -printed-pages-of-the-harvard-business-review/
26. www.macdrifter.com/2013/01/the-blog-comment-that-started-wordpress -link.html
27. www.wired.com/underwire/2012/03/ff_reddit/all/1

CHAPTER 3

1. www.bazaarvoice.com/blog/2011/11/22/unintended-benefits-how-social -media-can-help-people-with-autism/
2. daretocomment.com/dont-be-that-guy-in-social-media/
3. www.tedrubin.com/relationship-building-on-social-platforms/
4. www.youtube.com/watch?v=3mXuwTXet3s&feature=youtu.be
5. www.youtube.com/watch?v=1gOF6At68Hw
6. press.experian.com/United-States/Press-Release/experian-marketing -services-reveals-27-percent-of-time-spent-online-is-on-social-networking .aspx
7. technorati.com/social-media/article/social-media-use-at-work-is/
8. www.briansolis.com/2010/05/in-social-media-consumers-offer-rewards-to -deserving-brands/#comment-51060424
9. www.mpdailyfix.com/social-media-doesnt-connect-us-it-deepens-existing -connections/
10. adage.com/article/digitalnext/brands-plug-social-media-revolution /238235/

CHAPTER 4

1. twitter.com/be3d/status/61545040157229056
2. www.thedominoproject.com/2011/05/hashtags-for-books.html
3. gawker.com/5875241/let-us-all-come-together-to-improve-the-pr-industry -through-ridicule
4. www.urbandictionary.com/define.php?term=Humble%20Brag
5. twitter.com/petecashmore/status/195660905600651264
6. www.towson.edu/main/discovertowson/brianstelter.asp
7. www.nytimes.com/2006/11/20/business/media/20newser.html?_r=2&hp &ex=1164085200&en=c59846000bdadb8b&ei=5094&partner=homepage&
8. www.bazaarvoice.com/blog/2011/07/14/motivation-matters-new-research -on-the-psychology-of-sharing/
9. www.clarkkentslunchbox.com/
10. www.theunlost.com/

11. www.bazaarvoice.com/blog/2012/02/07/interview-how-kate-spade-uses
-social-to-live-colorfully-part-1/

CHAPTER 5

1. www.cbs.com/shows/undercover_boss/about/
2. www.minyanville.com/special-features/articles/undercover-boss-stock
-charts-share-prices/3/10/2011/id/33207
3. www.nypost.com/p/entertainment/tv/tock_boys_WQcF1NkQxbjq8
HIARJLHaI
4. articles.businessinsider.com/2011-04-18/strategy/29958189_1_leo
-apotheker-business-advice-job-title
5. www.forrester.com/rb/Research/2011_social_technographics%26%23174%
3B_for_business_technology_buyers/q/id/58564/t/2
6. www.slideshare.net/Tomtrendstream/globalwebindex-b2b-social-media
-strategy-2011
7. www.deloitte.com/view/en_US/us/About/Leadership/1fe8be4ad25e7310V
gnVCM1000001956f00aRCRD.htm
8. www.examiner.com/article/kobe-bryant-china-star-racks-up-followers-on
-blogging-site
9. www.npr.org/2011/10/24/141663195/what-is-the-basis-for-corporate
-personhood
10. www.convinceandconvert.com/social-media-strategy/social-pros-podcast
-justin-levy-citrix-online/
11. www.forbes.com/sites/shelisrael/2012/03/14/sm-thought-leaders-citis
-frank-eliason/
12. www.brandfog.com/CEOSocialMediaSurvey/BRANDfog_2012_CEO
_Survey.pdf
13. www.huffingtonpost.com/2012/05/24/barack-obama-twitter-chat_n
_1544215.html
14. www.digitaldaya.com/epetition.php?id_petition=69
15. www.forbes.com/sites/jeannemeister/2012/10/05/millennialmindse/
16. www.theworld.org/2013/01/uzbekistan-karimova/
17. customerevangelists.typepad.com/blog/2006/05/charting_wiki_p.html
18. www.nngroup.com/articles/participation-inequality/
19. www.ceo.com/social/#ceoid=prce313
20. www.bazaarvoice.com/cmo-club
21. tvnz.co.nz/national-news/broadband-holding-us-back-internet-nz-boss
-4733975
22. www.worcestermusicfestival.co.uk/features/meet-the-musicians/view
-musician/?nid=172
23. www.stephenfry.com/2012/02/26/wellington/single-page/
24. www.mediabistro.com/alltwitter/digital-journalism_b24440

25. www.poynter.org/how-tos/digital-strategies/163019/branded-journalists
    -battle-newsroom-regulations/
26. www.stephenfry.com/2012/02/26/wellington/single-page/
27. www.pewinternet.org/~/media//Files/Reports/2012/PIP_Privacy
    _management_on_social_media_sites_022412.pdf
28. gigaom.com/mobile/the-new-private-social-networks-were-trying-to
    -build-the-home/
29. aplusk.posterous.com/twitter-management
30. www.businessesgrow.com/2012/09/25/should-you-out-source-your-tweets/
31. blog.hubspot.com/blog/tabid/6307/bid/32208/Social-Media-Outsourcing
    -Increases-128-in-Two-Years-New-Report.aspx
32. www.nytimes.com/2012/07/19/fashion/celebrities-are-leaving-twitter.html
33. www.webpronews.com/greek-olympian-banned-for-racist-tweet-thinks
    -her-punishment-was-excessive-2012-07
34. sports.yahoo.com/blogs/tennis-busted-racquet/rebecca-marino-quits
    -tennis-because-bullying-social-media-175955476—ten.html
35. www.thestar.com/sports/tennis/2013/02/20/rebecca_marino_quits
    _tennis_following_cyberbullying_incidents.html
36. www.celebuzz.com/2012-08-30/leann-rimes-was-cyber-bullied-before
    -checking-into-rehab-exclusive/
37. bostonherald.com/inside_track/inside_track/2012/09/post_rehab_leann
    _rimes_shines
38. www.complex.com/tech/2012/11/the-100-biggest-twitter-fails-of-all-time
    /lance-armstrong-phone-number
39. venturebeat.com/2010/09/24/angelgate-cracks-wide-open-as-secret
    -meeting-attendees-bicker/
40. www.nypost.com/p/news/local/full_transcript_of_weiner_news
    _conference_JxlqpgCFcbffrWKKcwsyLL#ixzz1Obf7WfgT
41. www.complex.com/tech/2012/11/the-100-biggest-twitter-fails-of-all
    -time/spike-lee-dangerous-retweet
42. www.inquisitr.com/54986/bow-wow-drunk-driving-tweet/

CHAPTER 6

1. www.economist.com/node/21559334
2. www.pressgazette.co.uk/node/47497
3. www.guardian.co.uk/media/greenslade+sir-ray-tindle
4. www.bazaarvoice.com/blog/2011/07/13/your-customers-have-egos-and
   -that%E2%80%99s-great-for-you/
5. www.merriam-webster.com/dictionary/flattery
6. www.bazaarvoice.com/resources/research/get-them-talking-how
   -growing-participation-chains-will-grow-sales
7. cdixon.org/2012/09/11/vanity-milestones/

8. www.bazaarvoice.com/blog/2011/07/14/motivation-matters-new-research-on-the-psychology-of-sharing/

9. daretocomment.com/social-self-importance-why-content-curation-will-never-be-king/

10. images.fastcompany.com/Vivald-iPartners_Social-Currency.pdf

11. www.bazaarvoice.com/blog/2011/07/13/your-customers-have-egos-and-that%E2%80%99s-great-for-you/

CHAPTER 7

1. www.bazaarvoice.com/talking-to-strangers-millennials-trust-people-over-brands

2. trendwatching.com/trends/presumers/

3. www.economist.com/node/18114221

4. sloanreview.mit.edu/the-magazine/2011-fall/53105/the-age-of-the-consumer-innovator/

5. www.cnn.com/2012/06/22/living/customer-service-social-media/index.html

6. closeourloan.wordpress.com/

7. consumerist.com/2012/11/20/directv-says-it-will-credit-accounts-of-customers-with-rebooting-tivos/

8. www.edelmandigital.com/2011/02/14/why-millennials-matter-to-every-brand/

9. www.nytimes.com/2011/09/29/fashion/fashion-bloggers-get-agents.html?_r=1&pagewanted=print&

10. According to Compete.com on 12/07/12

11. www.idioplatform.com/american-express-open-forum-content-marketing-for-small-businesses/

12. www.bazaarvoice.com/blog/2010/06/17/urban-outfitters%E2%80%99-rules-to-social-marketing/

13. www.charlotteobserver.com/2013/02/08/3842194/doritos-ad-gets-charlotte-director.html

14. www.usatoday.com/story/money/business/2013/01/14/super-bowl-ad-costs-kantar-media/1833807/

15. apps.facebook.com/crashthesuperbowl/

16. www.buzzfeed.com/jackstuef/the-man-behind-comfortablysmug-hurricane-sandys

17. www.nbcnews.com/technology/technolog/man-who-made-false-tweet-about-sandy-apologizes-could-face-1C6807076

18. gofwd.tumblr.com/post/34623466723/twitter-is-a-truth-machine

19. irevolution.net/2012/11/14/percentage-tweets-response/

20. govwin.com/ehalperin_blog/hurricane-sandy-fema-social-media/732887

21. www.macrumors.com/2012/01/24/apple-has-an-unboxing-room-to-test-hundreds-of-variants-of-their-product-packaging/

22. www.npr.org/templates/transcript/transcript.php?storyId=164742426

23. adage.com/article/digital/study-reach-organic-facebook-posts-engagement /238365/

CHAPTER 8

1. www.whitehouse.gov/blog/2012/09/04/we-people-3-million-signatures -later
2. www.nextgov.com/emerging-tech/2012/11/residents-all-50-states-have -filed-secession-petitions/59556/
3. lanceingle.com/playground/
4. mashable.com/category/stop-online-piracy-act/
5. mediamatters.org/blog/2012/01/13/study-sopa-coverage-no-match-for-kim -kardashian/186175
6. venturebeat.com/2011/12/24/godaddy-domain-loss/
7. www.people-press.org/2012/01/24/cruise-ship-accident-election-top -publics-interest/
8. en.wikipedia.org/wiki/Protests_against_SOPA_and_PIPA#January_18
9. www.fastcompany.com/3005070/social-vs-washington-old-boy-network -case-study-keystone-xl-pipeline

CHAPTER 9

1. blog.datasift.com/2013/02/04/how-brands-fared-socially-during-the -super-bowl/
2. mashable.com/2011/12/07/facebook-faces-emotion/
3. www.aimclearblog.com/2013/01/09/inbound-pr-pulling-media-mindshare -with-content-big-data/
4. lindsayrobertson.tumblr.com/post/330892541/the-dos-and-donts-of -online-publicity-for-some-reason
5. www.socialmediaexplorer.com/social-media-marketing/foxes-hedgehogs -and-social-media-myopia/
6. www.youtube.com/watch?v=4jkwRHe9B4s
7. money.cnn.com/2012/10/17/technology/social/binders-full-of-women -domain/index.html
8. theweek.com/article/index/240134/how-poland-spring-squandered-its -marco-rubio-moment
9. www.leandomainsearch.com/trends/explore?q=rubio

CHAPTER 10

1. blog.linkedin.com/2012/10/02/follow-people/
2. techcrunch.com/2012/10/11/facebook-custom-audience-ads/

CHAPTER 11

1. www.youtube.com/watch?v=Rti5vrjp5aI&lc=RUH3-OeR9JcISBSRMeZ_bbOt1Io_vQSuOtaYFLyh1dg
2. twitter.com/kissane/status/292316628413202432
3. twitter.com/kissane/status/292318497210527744
4. www.entrepreneur.com/blog/225651#
5. www.nytimes.com/2013/01/31/technology/facebook-earnings.html?_r=0
6. www.mobilemarketer.com/cms/news/social-networks/14550.html
7. allfacebook.com/study-13-of-americans-use-facebook-in-the-bathroom_b30108
8. money.cnn.com/2013/04/08/technology/social/facebook-paid-messages-trial/index.html
9. money.cnn.com/2013/04/08/technology/social/facebook-paid-messages-trial/index.html
10. support.twitter.com/articles/119135-faqs-about-verified-accounts#
11. www.briancuban.com/how-i-got-verified-on-twitter/
12. www.theverge.com/2013/2/1/3941014/bogus-twitter-account-promises-verification-snags-22000-hopeful

INDEX

ABOUT THE AUTHOR

an Greenleigh turns data, ideas, and relationships into reach and influence through content and social strategy. His words and ideas have been featured in *Harvard Business Review, AdAge, Adweek, Ragan, Seth Godin's The Domino Project*, and elsewhere. He writes and speaks on a wide range of topics, including changing consumer-brand relationships, the convergence of personal identities, and the radically shifting landscapes of access and influence. Visit daretocomment.com and follow him at @be3d.